mine

River Teeth Literary Nonfiction Prize
Daniel Lehman and Joe Mackall, SERIES EDITORS

The *River Teeth* Literary Nonfiction Prize is awarded to the best work of literary nonfiction submitted to the annual contest sponsored by *River Teeth: A Journal of Nonfiction Narrative*.

Also available in the *River Teeth* Literary Nonfiction Prize series:

Rough Crossing: An Alaskan Fisherwoman's Memoir
    by Rosemary McGuire
The Girls in My Town: Essays by Angela Morales

mine

essays

sarah viren

University of New Mexico Press — Albuquerque

Library of Congress Cataloging-in-Publication Data
Names: Viren, Sarah, 1979– author.
Title: Mine: Essays / Sarah Viren.
Description: First edition. | Albuquerque: University of New Mexico Press,
    [2018]
Identifiers: LCCN 2017036425 (print) | LCCN 2017043458 (e-book) |
    ISBN 9780826359551 (e-book) | ISBN 9780826359544 (softcover: acid-free
    paper)
Classification: LCC PS3622.I73 (e-book) | LCC PS3622.I73 A6 2018 (print) |
    DDC 814/.6—dc23
LC record available at https://lccn.loc.gov/2017036425

Cover photograph courtsey of the author
Designed by Felicia Cedillos
Composed in Palatino LT Std 10.24/14

contents

how should I define the limits of my concern
the boundary between mine and not-mine

—MONICA YOUN

MY MURDERER'S FUTON

THE FUTON WAS cheaply made. Faux-brass knobs accented its armrests, and its lacquered wood finish had begun to chip away. Its metal rib cage pushed through a thin white mattress, kneading my back while I slept at night. In the morning I would wake to the slight stench of mildew from the cushioning by my head. Lying there I wondered if he, too, had been bothered by the smell.

Beside the futon I kept his alarm clock, and in the kitchen were his table and chairs. They were light-colored, likely maple, and some days I could almost see him there, sitting just as I did, alone in the morning, pouring myself cereal, staring at the wall molding. The TV I am certain he used, flipping through the channels until he found a stock and finance show. That is what was on the morning of the killing, at least according to court testimony. In my apartment his TV sat above his VCR on a metal bookshelf that my mother had bought me when she came to visit and realized that I had nothing of my own in my new place. She had bought me a Target standing lamp as well, but it was his white lamp that I plugged in near the front door.

When I got home at night after work and turned it on, it was his light that exposed my home to me.

Robert Durst was not a murderer, at least not legally speaking. He was a billion-dollar real estate heir who went missing from his New York apartment in 2000. He showed up on Galveston Island in Texas some time later, transformed, albeit unconvincingly, into a mute woman named Dorothy Ciner. Rather than talk, they say, he would write down messages on a piece of paper. He rented a studio apartment from a tall German named Klaus and lived quietly on the island for almost a year.

Then one September afternoon in 2001, a father and son were fishing in Galveston Bay when they happened upon the dismembered torso of a man in a garbage bag. In those same waters, police later found five black plastic bags containing a .22 caliber automatic pistol, the plastic cover for a bow saw, and two human arms and legs wrapped in old copies of the *Galveston County Daily News*. The newspapers had Durst's address on the mailing label. Nine days later Durst was arrested for the murder of his sixty-one-year-old neighbor, Morris Black.

Police claimed Durst had been living in Galveston, disguised as a woman, while hiding out from officers in California who wanted to question him about another murder: the shooting of his best friend Susan Berman on Christmas Eve of 2000. Before she was killed, Berman had been about to talk to police regarding the mysterious disappearance of Durst's first wife, Kathie, twenty-three years earlier. But today Durst cannot be called a murderer. In fact my calling his futon a murderer's futon is quite possibly slander, at least legally speaking. Still, that is what I called it: my murderer's futon.

I moved to Galveston from Florida in 2003, three years after

Durst had arrived. Galveston is an island south of Houston that was once nicknamed the Wall Street of the South, though these days it is better known as one of three things: a cheap beach resort, the name of a Glen Campbell song, or the site of one of the deadliest natural disasters in United States history. On a September day in 1900, a Category 4 hurricane rose from the ocean and smothered the thirty miles of paved roads, stately houses, electric streetcars, and beachfront hotels that were Galveston Island. When the hurricane's waves retreated, they left behind close to eight thousand dead bodies and barren flat land where mansions once held sway. The island never regained its charm. And that feeling of revoked regality, that hint of death, was still palpable when I moved there. A friend of mine, a poet, came to visit me once and said she could taste ghosts in the air. Sensible people said nonsensical things like that all the time in Galveston.

I had moved there for a job. After graduating from college I decided that all I really wanted was to be a newspaper reporter. My first try was with a weekly paper called the *Boca Beacon* on a small island in Florida—a place where everyone drove golf carts and "the news" often meant covering dog shows and performances by retired Whiffenpoof singers. So when an editor at the *Galveston County Daily News*, a friend of a photographer I knew in Florida, called with a job offer at his paper, I said yes without hesitation, quit my Florida island job, sold all my things, and moved alone to start a new life in Galveston.

I found my apartment through a classified ad posted by a tall German named Klaus. It was a one-bedroom shotgun that hung from the side of a renovated Victorian house a few blocks from the historic downtown. Two blocks away was a bed-and-breakfast run by a former Playboy bunny. Ten blocks south of that you hit the Seawall and beyond that the beach. In the

3

mornings prostitutes walked the ocean line, offering what one Houston weekly had called "a blow job on the way to work." In the evenings they were replaced by Segways and packs of pasty families. The rest of the island was filled with empty cotton sheds and port piers, strip malls and T-shirt shops, renovated lofts, new swanky restaurants, and too many abandoned beach houses.

When I met Klaus what I noticed first was how perfectly square his jaw was and how tightly he had knotted the red handkerchief around his head. He always wore that handkerchief and, together with his tool belt, it gave him the look of a pirate moonlighting as a carpenter, which was not altogether inappropriate given that Galveston was once a famous hideout for the French pirate Jean Lafitte.

Klaus was close to fifty and had owned a chain of beauty shops in Houston before selling them and investing that money in Galveston real estate, which everyone said was about to boom. In 2000 he rented one of his apartments to a deaf woman named Dorothy Ciner. It was several miles from the one he would rent to me three years later. But after the arrest, after the police confiscated all of Robert Durst's belongings, after they ripped up the floorboards in his rented apartment and drilled through the walls looking for evidence, they gave Durst's confiscated furniture to Klaus, and Klaus moved it to an extra garage a few blocks from the apartment that I would later rent from him.

"Don't worry. He did not live in *your* apartment," Klaus assured me in his thick German accent after he told me the story.

We were standing in the doorway of that garage, our eyes adjusting to the darkness. After signing the lease I'd mentioned that I had no furniture, and Klaus had said he could give me some for free—as long as I didn't mind who the previous owner was. I said I didn't, and he told me to follow him. In the darkness I could make out the shape of a pale kitchen table in the corner of the garage. It supported a TV, a VCR, and a Time Warner cable box. The contour of a futon slowly came into focus. It sat upright—almost rapt—facing the stacked electronics.

"You sure he won't mind?" I asked Klaus, suddenly hesitant. Durst's murder trial was underway in the county courthouse a few blocks away from where we were standing. He had been charged with first-degree murder, but he was claiming self-defense. I imagined Durst on the witness stand, and it suddenly seemed wrong to take his belongings without his permission. Later, people who learned about my furniture would tell me that taking Durst's things was wrong for other reasons. "How could you?" they would ask, mouths agape. "He's a murderer!" But I've never been sentimental or superstitious. Rather than being disgusted or scared by the furniture, I was curious. But I still didn't want to steal from someone— murderer or not.

"He is going to have a lot of bigger things to worry about if he ever gets out of there," Klaus assured me. "Besides, he owes me lots of money, Robert Durst."

Then, looking over at the futon, he added, "You think you can relax on that, huh?"

He cracked a slight smile. Without answering I walked over and picked up one end, and together we loaded the futon into Klaus's baby-blue Suburban. In three trips between the garage and my apartment we moved the remainder of Durst's belongings into my new home.

I knew very little about Robert Durst before I began sleeping on his futon. I learned more through Google searches and by reading the articles about his trial that ran almost every day in the *Galveston County Daily News* during my first few weeks on the job. I learned that Robert Durst is the grandson of Joseph Durst, a Jewish immigrant from the Austro-Hungarian region who, according to legend, arrived in America with only three dollars sewn into his coat lapel and later made millions buying up property in New York City. The Durst Organization is now a billion-dollar company that oversees more than 9.5 million square feet of real estate in Manhattan.

Durst was born in 1943, a year after my father. At age seven he says he watched his mother's deadly fall—some say suicide—from the roof of the family's Scarsdale home. In the following years Durst grew into something of a rich-kid rebel, hobnobbing at Studio 54 and trying scream therapy with John Lennon. After college he ran a health food store called "All Good Things" in Vermont with his first wife, Kathie. The 2010 fictionalization of his life starring Ryan Gosling as Durst and Kirsten Dunst as his wife takes the name of that store as its title. The 2014 HBO documentary series about Durst by the same director chose the name *The Jinx* instead—because Durst claims that he's jinxed. He's not a murderer, he says, but the victim of a string of bad luck.

Life started to become complicated for Durst in January of 1982 when Kathie disappeared. Some of her friends blamed Durst. They said the two hadn't been getting along, that he pulled her hair and sometimes hit her. Kathie had been finishing her medical degree then and was often absent. Durst, in turn, was controlling of her free time. But he said he was innocent. He plastered $15,000 reward posters with Kathie's picture across New York City. Later, when he started adopting other people's identities, he sometimes used his wife's name. Another name he borrowed was Diana Winn. And another was Morris Black.

Dorothy Ciner was the name of an old high school classmate of his in Scarsdale. When Durst became Dorothy he donned a blonde wig and glasses taped together at the front. He is a slight man with fine features, so sometimes he could pull off the disguise. Other times not. When asked to describe Dorothy Ciner in court, Klaus said, "She looked like a middle-aged woman with a flat chest. I felt sorry for the poor thing."

A week after I moved to Galveston I was given the police beat. This assignment meant covering crime in four small towns just north of the island. It also meant picking up the phone every day and calling four gruff-voiced men in brown suits with badges, all of whom went only by *chief* and periodically asked me, "Hey, whatever happened to Scott, anyway?" Scott, my cop-beat predecessor, had been promoted to covering the Durst trial full-time. Scott liked pro-wrestling. He called the hit-and-run deaths of thirteen-year-olds on Schwinn bicycles "juvenile autopeds." The police chiefs missed him.

The largest of these men presided over a town split in half by an old farm road. His police department was the size of two double-wides. We met in person for the first time when I was writing a story about a change to local gun laws. The town's council had outlawed shooting guns within city limits. I stopped by his office to get his opinion on the new restriction.

"Take a seat; he'll come get you," the woman behind a scratched plexiglass window in the police station's waiting room told me. I paced the narrow corridor, looking at the safety information tacked to the wood-paneled walls. The intermittent crackle of the police radio interrupted chatter between the front desk woman and a dispatcher.

"Sarah," the chief finally wheezed, opening the main waiting-room door with a swoosh. The safety pamphlets flapped. He took my outstretched hand in his well-padded one. It was a quick shake with no accompanying slap on the back. I wondered what kind of greeting Scott used to get.

Compared to the rest of the station, the chief's office was sprawling. Everything—walls, carpet, furniture—was a deep, earthy brown. A massive oak desk anchored all of this. After gesturing me toward a small chair facing that desk, the chief leaned back in his leather chair with a contented sigh. Having the desk between us clearly put him at ease.

"Chief, I heard about the shooting ban passed by city council and was wondering what you think. Have you had any problems in the past with people firing off guns around town?"

He didn't meet my eye.

"Yeah, they did pass that, didn't they?" he said. He blinked and picked up a coffee mug. Without drinking, he replaced the cup on some folded papers and then mumbled something about duck hunters and people protecting their property. I nodded and wrote.

"Do you know anyone—" I paused, "—anyone I could talk to about this? Maybe a homeowner or hunter who was upset by the change?"

The chief could sense my hesitancy, my lack of experience, my gender. He shook his head.

"What's going on with that murderer you got down there?" he said instead.

He was talking about Durst, of course. All the chiefs asked about him. It was their favorite subject. They would press me for the latest on the trial and then opine on the correct sentencing "that New Yorker" should face.

"How anyone could have taken him for a woman I don't

know," he mused. "Can you imagine what he looked like all dressed up?" Then he laughed, or wheezed, and waited for my response.

Like most of the officers I'd met, the chief was more fascinated by Durst having dressed in drag than by his alleged crime. It was both exotic and terrifying. It simultaneously confirmed their prejudices and freaked them out, which I think they secretly liked. But for me, Durst's redeeming quality was the fact that he had cross-dressed. It made him an outsider, which was something I understood—as a journalist, as a woman, and, though I told none of the chiefs, as a lesbian living and working in a place where local politicians still remained in the closet, where a church just up the road would later hold a conference to "help" gays turn straight, where a sweet old lady I opened the door for at a voting booth once told me proudly she had come to cast a ballot in favor of the state's anti-gay marriage amendment. All this, coupled with the fact that I slept on Durst's futon, ate at his kitchen table, watched his TV, meant that I found myself taking Durst's side, in small ways, in brief moments like this one where someone like the chief asked me to call Durst a freak.

In my silence the chief picked up his coffee mug. Part of your job as a reporter is to make yourself likeable. Likable people get information from people like the chief. But I couldn't do it. I wouldn't come to the rescue of Robert Durst, but I couldn't mock him either.

"Yep," I finally said, "he sure is the talk."

The chief took a sip of his coffee. I pulled out my pen again. The desk between us was vast.

Those first few months I knew almost no one in Galveston, and so on weekends or after work I would spend hours on the futon, reading, sleeping, or writing. To get out of the house I would walk down to the port and pay five bucks to watch *The Great Storm*, a twenty-minute documentary film about the hurricane that played every hour on the hour except on Thursdays. The theater was in an old brick building above a seafood restaurant called Willie G's. In the gift shop they sold coffee table books full of photos from Galveston before the storm and pirate doll keychains of Jean Lafitte.

What I loved about watching *The Great Storm* was the sense of inevitability. Just as in Erik Larson's book *Isaac's Storm*, written from the perspective of the weatherman who failed to predict the hurricane's approach, the film stresses the hubris of Galveston in those pre-hurricane years. It opens with sepia-toned photos of a broad-boulevarded city lined with mansions, and then a booming voice, imitating one of the city's founding fathers, reads a quote: "Galveston, with a population of forty thousand, is the most important seaport in Texas and *nothing* can retard its commercial prosperity." Similarly boastful quotes follow one after the other, lauding Galveston's once "fine buildings," its former grand opera house, its "system of electric street cars," its beach that is the "finest in the world," and its future that "cannot easily be foretold"—all of this accompanied by the sound of piano music and chitter-chatter meant to represent the thousands of wealthy tourists who would travel to the city in the late 1800s and stay in its massive Beach Hotel that faced the open waterfront. But following such jubilance came a deep silence. A darkening of the screen. The tapping of Morse code keys. And then the mounting sounds of a storm whirling.

I probably watched the island be destroyed half a dozen times in my first few months in Galveston. Meanwhile Robert Durst slept on a cot in the county jail four blocks away. His trial lasted seven weeks, and Scott reported each day on the proceedings. A psychiatrist testified that Durst had Asperger syndrome and that this explains why he so often reacted coldly to the tragedies around him. The defense argued that he was a sociopath. Klaus testified. So did the man who had found Morris Black's body in the Galveston Bay.

Near the end of the trial Durst took the stand. He explained his difficult upbringing to the jury and said that after his wife's disappearance he had started smoking too much pot, drinking too much, and had developed bulimia. He said that he moved to Galveston because he "did not want to be Robert Durst anymore." So he tried—but failed—to become someone else.

In Galveston he rented an apartment from Klaus for three hundred dollars a month and became friends with his neighbor Morris Black, a man known for his violent temper. They watched TV together and went target shooting on Pelican Island. They both liked bourbon. But then Black started firing off Durst's gun inside his apartment and using a spare key to get inside and watch Durst's TV—later my TV—without his permission. One morning, after walking the seawall until 6:00 a.m., Durst said he came home to find Black in his apartment again watching his TV. He went for his gun, he said, but Morris Black already had it. They struggled over it, and at some point it went off, shooting Black in the head.

Durst said he didn't remember much of the dismembering. He bought a bottle of whiskey and drank it while he sawed. He said he didn't go to the police because he knew they wouldn't believe him. "I kept going over the situation in my mind," he said. "Morris was shot in the face with my gun, in my apartment, and I had rented this apartment disguised as a woman."

On Durst's last day on the stand, the prosecution pressed him to remember more details, and eventually he admitted that he could recall one part: "I remember like I was looking down on something and I was swimming in blood and I kept spitting up and spitting up and I don't know what is real and I don't know what is not real," he said.

Reading his words, I couldn't help but notice his use of the present tense. It was like whatever had happened was still happening—the distinction between then and now erased. And with this erasure, or perhaps before it, we also lose the border between the real and the unreal, between one life and another.

Less than a week later the jury found Durst not guilty. His eyes widened when the verdict was read, and then he hugged each of his six-member legal team. Afterward jurors said they weren't convinced the killing was premeditated. The case against Durst had been weakened by one fact: no one ever found Black's head.

And without Black's head there was no way to tell how close Durst had been when he shot his neighbor, at what angle, or from what direction. In other words, there was no way to know if we should believe his story or not.

Journalists are supposed to uncover the truth. In those early days of working at newspapers, this is how I thought of my profession. But putting yourself in charge of uncovering the truth can also feel like an unraveling. It feels like the truth is always there, just out of reach, waiting to be revealed. Every time I interviewed a local politician. Every time I called one of those police chiefs. Every time I came home and recognized one of Durst's belongings among mine and thought, without really thinking, that I knew a secret about him, something that would change the course of the trial and, later, after he was found not guilty, something that would change the course of his life, something that would finally reveal who he really was and what had really happened to him when he lived among all the furniture that I later took as my own.

I've read about women who become obsessed with killers. After Scott Peterson was convicted of killing his pregnant wife, he got numerous marriage proposals in jail from women he had never met. Groupies of Ted Bundy attended his trial, giggling when he looked their way and smiled. Even John Wayne Gacy, who was gay, got jailhouse love letters from female fans. But my infatuation with Robert Durst was different. I was not in love with him, but I did feel like I understood him. I didn't see him as many likely did: in a pool of blood and a tight-fitting dress. Instead I imagined him as he might have been in Galveston before the killing: numb from the pot he habitually smoked, depressed, and alone. I pictured him at the end of his day, dragging himself up the steps to his apartment, a dress tugging against his prickly legs, a scarf covering his bob-wigged head. Was he tired of pretending? Was he crazy with reality?

After the acquittal, police held Durst ten months longer on bond jumping and charges of tampering with evidence—the evidence being Black's body—and during that time he was locked up in the county jail just blocks from where I lived. His lawyer said he kept a photo of his wife Kathie on the bedside table. I never saw him in person, but I sometimes thought, in that midafternoon musing sort of way, that I might pay him a visit. "Hello, I have your furniture," I would say, as if he had been wondering and worrying about his futon and TV for the last three years. Or perhaps he would seek me out, rushing to find his belongings after being let out of jail. I would be sweeping the kitchen on a Saturday afternoon and hear the knock on the door. "I'm here for my stuff," Durst would say, his features frozen like they were in pictures on the newspaper's front page. These fantasies were almost crisp in their simplicity, like

Durst and I were longtime business partners, always aware that we had one last transaction to settle before going our separate ways.

Nearly a year after I moved to Galveston, local authorities reached a plea deal with Durst on his outstanding charges. He was released and transferred by the FBI to a Pennsylvania jail for sentencing on a separate concealed-weapons charge. Slowly the talk about him around Galveston began to die down. I was moved from the police beat to covering city hall. I met new friends and purchased a mattress and box spring—moving Durst's futon to the living room, where I kept it upright and accented it with green throw pillows and an apple blanket my mother had made for me six years earlier.

But I still took naps on Durst's futon for some time after that. Throwing down a book or the last part of a magazine article, I would turn on to my belly, push my elbow against the crux of the futon mattress, and dig my way into afternoon sleep. Almost without fail, when I woke ten or twenty minutes later I would be lost for a moment. Nose mashed against white cushioning, my mind would touch fleetingly on the slip of a life not quite mine—like that moment when you turn the last page of a good novel and flip back again quickly, just to make sure it really came to an end.

One morning around this time I was eating oatmeal at Durst's kitchen table when I noticed that it was extendable. Peering underneath, looking for the latches, I pushed the two leaves apart and suddenly saw something dark along the twin edges. There were small, almost-black stains, like dried drips of some liquid that had fallen between the table's center crack. Immediately I thought of dried blood. I pushed the leaves wider apart and peered between them, brushing my finger lightly across the stains. I considered calling the police or someone at the newspaper. I imagined that this blood would be the clue that would unravel everything. What I meant by *everything*, though, I had no idea. Standing there, short of breath, I felt so close to a moment that was not my own. But then I looked closer at the table, and I realized the stains were not blood but mildew. Galveston is old and wet. Mold grows everywhere.

MY CATCH

THE FIRST TIME I went fishing was in high school. We skipped class and went to the Hillsborough River, got high, and practiced casting lures into the water. I looked over at my best friend, bare tan legs swinging off the dock, just above the tea-leaf water, and I wanted to touch her. Our boyfriends tittered behind us. And we never caught a thing.

The second time I went fishing was with my college girl-friend, a woman named Jennifer who was slim-waisted and lightly freckled, and who I took to calling Penny because she was bright and shiny, but also solid and uncomplicated in a way that I liked back then. She sought out bass on different parts of that same river in Tampa. We would steal out from our bed early in the morning for what looked like Tai Chi by the banks. Cast. Reel. Reel. Reel. Cast. Wait.

Later she took me on a boat with her father on a lake in north Texas. I caught bass then, too, but preferred drinking cold Coors Lights and watching the dark shadows of the fish on the boat's sonar system, the sun dance of my bobber on the surface of the lake, and, most of all, the ease with which Penny, my bass fisherwoman, would cast and reel, and then after a long stretch of silence, catch.

"Babe," she'd turn to look at me, her eyes wide and blue like a north Texas sky. "Wanna learn to how to take out a hook?"

The last time I went fishing was after I left her. And that time everything was different. It was at night, and we weren't on a river or a lake but in the dark waters of a bay off an island called Boca Grande in southwest Florida where a fish called the tarpon is legendary and almost everyone has a tale of catching a big one.

Boca Grande literally means "Big Mouth." The mouth in this case is a metaphorical yawn where the waters of the Gulf of Mexico meet the Charlotte Harbor at the island's southern tip, a spot where shrimp and sharks and tarpon like to congregate and feed. Today some tarpon fishermen refer to that stretch of water as the cafeteria bowl of the Gulf because there are so many tarpon eating and spawning there.

The Calusa discovered Boca Grande sometime in the first century and included it in their fishing empire along Florida's west coast. Then the Spaniards arrived, and the Calusa slowly died off or were killed. A railroad came to Boca Grande, and by the early 1900s the island was an important port for the distribution of phosphate as well as a second home for rich people who made money off the phosphate and who liked to fish tarpon for sport in their free time. The town square grew to include a gourmet grocery store, restaurants with white table clothes, and a Lilly Pulitzer boutique shop. The Du Ponts bought summer houses and opened a small school for the locals. Katharine Hepburn went for her morning swim on the island's bayside. And at some point someone told the Bushes, and next thing you know Jenna and Barbara Bush were partying at the local bar alongside a life-size sculpture of a tarpon made from beer bottle caps by one of the many local artists who shared the island with Du Ponts and Bushes and former Yale Whiffenpoof singers.

I showed up on the island in 2002, six months after graduating from college and a month after everything fell apart with my bass fisherwoman. I brought with me a three-page résumé detailing my experience: espresso making, bowling-alley-burger flipping, paper filing, waitressing, book-order processing, and publicity seeking. The reporter at the local newspaper, the *Boca Beacon*, had quit suddenly after a fight with the editor, and a friend of a friend happened to be the daughter of the newspaper's publisher. She recommended that I apply.

"I want to be a writer," I told Gary, the editor. He had chubby fingers and smooth, tanned skin that reminded me of a river stone. He nodded, skimmed my credentials, and said he thought I had potential. He offered me twelve dollars an hour, no insurance, and I accepted without hesitation. I had just moved out of the apartment that I'd shared with Penny for two years, and I was living in someone's renovated garage. More than a job, I needed change.

My professional duties commenced the next day: a weekly profile of an "influential" resident or local employee, a weekly brief on any local crime, and regular stories about new businesses, property taxes, golf-cart accidents, iguana infestations, beach erosion, bridge-toll hikes, and, once, the appearance on the beach of a dead thirty-foot sperm whale. Less than a month after starting at the paper, Gary informed me of one more requirement.

"Tarpon is king here," he said. "You've got to catch one."

The story of the tarpon begins one hundred million years ago. Wade back through a dozen climate cycles—through the Neogene and Paleogene periods, through the Oligocene and Eocene epochs—and there you'll find its origin. One of the oldest and largest fish in the sea, its birth looks like a mating between the whooping crane and the crocodile. A strange dance: half air, half water, scale mixing with feather mixing with flesh and fin. Because one important thing about tarpon is this: they breathe. They gulp air, just like you and me. In the tarpon, organs like lungs filter oxygen in concert with gills, sharp and bloody.

The scientists tell us another story of the tarpon. Once, they say, these fish swam in giant herds everywhere in the Gulf of Mexico. Their lives began somewhere south, either in Florida or Mexico where the waters are warm. But tarpon are swimmers, and as the weather warms each summer they slither up the Gulf of Mexico on both sides—Mexico to Texas and maybe Louisiana; the Florida Keys to Pensacola and then toward the great Mississippi—chasing mullet and shrimp and crabs. This migration has been their annual marathon for one hundred million years. And for years we killed them when they reached our nearest fishing holes. Yet they survived.

Because they gulp air. Because they are as big as we are. Because of their eyes.

"They stare at you," a tarpon guide told me once with a sort of conspiratorial glee. "They lock eyes."

Indeed, they were named for those eyes. Their Latin name is *Megalops atlanticus*, meaning "Big Eyes of the Atlantic." Silver King is their familiar name, a moniker evoked in fishing tournaments where dozens of beer bellies hop into skiffs to skim the ocean in midafternoon, plopping down crabs or jigs, trying to snag the biggest tarpon of the bunch. They call them *silver* because of the color of their scales—a sweet metallic blue that glimmers in sunlight—and *king* because of their royal authority. In some circles, tarpon are an addiction. They have ended marriages. They have killed those who love them, their silver-blue bodies flying from the water and, in a leap, slamming into a twenty-year-old holding a rod and reel, knocking him from this world to the next. Tiny Poseidons, they are.

But scientists prefer the *Megalops* reference.

"Their eyes are infrared," one told me after I asked him what it is about tarpon that makes them so unique. "They can see in the dark. This is a very ancient fish."

He had just published a book of studies on tarpon and hoped one day to count every tarpon that swims in the Gulf of Mexico.

"Too many people are killing them," he complained. "If only they understood their worth."

Because, while we have killed tarpon for years, not that long ago we began to kill too many. In Louisiana they speared them to death. In Mexico a mayor offered a truck for the biggest one. Others elsewhere were so poor and hungry they began killing the oily, bony fish for food.

But really, I wanted to tell the scientist, tarpon are killed because they have so much worth. There are people who value them so much they want to memorialize the fish. They kill them and hang them from the rafters of a dock for a picture. They kill them and mount their arcing, taxidermied bodies above the mantel in a lodge or hotel. They value the tarpon enough to want to make them theirs forever.

And therein lies the problem. This destructive form of admiration, maybe even love, is why there are now laws in every state prohibiting the killing of tarpon. We may fish them, yes, but after we have caught them we have to let them go.

On the day appointed for my tarpon catch, a fishing captain named Steve Futch arrived at the Boca Grande dock with his boat, *Lil' Priss*. It was two hours after sunset. Captain Futch had been tracking the tides, watching the movement of baitfish, and he decided this was the time. Close to midnight, he guaranteed, the mullet would be running, which meant the tarpon would be biting, which meant we would get our great catch.

We climbed on board: me in a hooded sweatshirt and cap to restrain my errant blonde hair that seemed attracted to the wind; Gary and his wife, Lynne; Rebecca, a tan, full-lipped advertising rep; and the newspaper's publisher, a short man named Dusty who had outfitted his island golf cart to look like a Harley Davidson. Rebecca and I each sat down in designated tarpon-fishing seats near the stern above a rumbling inboard motor. Rebecca crossed her long legs. Beside us Dusty sat on an ice chest, camera in hand. The newspaper had no staff photographer, so he filled that role as well.

"We need to capture your initiation," Dusty explained.

"Tarpon virgin," someone else poked.

"This is unlike any fishing you've done before," Captain Futch emphasized as he directed his boat toward the bay. Behind us a lazy halo of light encircled Boca Grande. The inky waves reflected moonlight the color of polished teaspoons. Rebecca's mouth flashed white at our captain, and I tried to smile, too, but I felt too nervous.

"Little ol' ladies the size of my pinky have reeled in tarpon twice their size," Captain Futch reassured me. "You'll be more than fine out here."

The first time we cast I watched my line disappear into the night. The bobber jiggled, already so different from ones I'd seen on the lake or on the river, where movement like that would mean a fish was already nibbling at my bait. Out there on the open water it signified nothing more than an ocean swaying against the night. I sipped from an Amstel Light, refocused my eyes on the orange sphere in the sea, and imagined a telephone line running from my rod, through the line, and down to the tarpon below.

The first pull, when it finally came, was so hard it jerked me present. My line morphed from slack to a natural force, like that fear that comes with a steep fall in a dream, knocking you awake just as your body loses weight.

All I could do was brace myself and yell. Captain Futch gunned the engine. Then just as quickly as it appeared, that tug of life vanished. My line went slack, my tarpon lost.

"Shit," Captain Futch sighed.

Dusty put down the camera. The water was so dark I couldn't see the waves.

I met my bass fisherwoman when I was eighteen. We happened to be at the same coffee shop one afternoon and started to talk about books. I said I loved *My Side of the Mountain* as a kid and she told me she had, too. We'd both read lots of Sylvia Plath, listened to lots of Tori Amos, and refused to eat meat. She had broad shoulders and big, blue eyes that locked on mine whenever I spoke. I felt dizzy, and she felt right.

My senior prom was a week later, and I invited her to the after party at a Motel 6. That night we kissed for the first time in a shared double bed with the lights out, my friends sleeping in the bed beside us or on the floor. The first time we made love was in my bedroom in my parents' suburban house. We kept quieting each other so that no one would hear us. Afterward we watched the moon rise over the swamp through the back window of my bedroom and talked about our ideal house.

"Mine would have a spiral staircase in the kitchen," I said. "And there would be at least one window seat where I could sit and read."

"I'd like a big front porch," she told me. "And a view of the woods with a river running down below."

I told my parents she was a new friend, but they knew better. When I finally came out, my mom's only response was, "You love her, don't you?" To this day my sister still asks about her. "She was so funny," she says. "She was like family to us."

She was a Texan and a college dropout who had joined the Air Force just to "get out of there," as she told me later. She smoked Virginia Slim Lights, almost always wore a baseball cap, and made wishes when the clock read 11:11. She taught me how to play pool, and I got her into Scrabble. Soon after we started dating I went to college and she was sent on three-month tours to Turkey, then Saudi Arabia, then Italy. We wrote long letters to each other filled with the kinds of things you say when you're that young and in love for the first time.

"I'm at a stoplight. It's raining. The rain reminds me of you," I wrote.

"Sometimes I whisper your name, *Sarah*, in the wind," she wrote back.

And then later, "I want you to see what I see and love it, too. But you can't, and that's not your fault. This silent roar inside me."

Each time we came back to each other after a period apart, the intensity I had felt for her was renewed. I stopped making new friends and spoke less and less with the ones I'd had for years. She told me I was her best friend and that she didn't need anyone else. We swore we were happiest when we were together. We swore it.

Once, we climbed on top of a strip mall and made love

against the parapet. I leaned into the sheet metal and concrete and she leaned into me, half standing, half falling. I looked up and watched the night sky until I felt her fill me. We cried that night, afterward. Or maybe it was another night. Because for a long while it felt like we were swimming together.

Until one day I realized I could no longer breathe.

After my first loss, Captain Futch showed me the crabs and demonstrated how to re-bait my hook.

"Try again," he sighed. "This time, don't pull so hard."

I held the reel in my hands and put the crab bait on my hook and cast it again into nothingness. I was sure I would lose the fish again. But after maybe twenty minutes I felt it. The pull was so unmistakable there was no time to pause. I yelled "Fish on" as I had been told to do, and Captain Futch again gunned *Lil' Priss* and, finally, my tarpon latched on.

The fight that followed—because they still call fishing for tarpon a fight—really was like a martial art. I reeled in the line, folding it upon itself like a kite that's run with the wind, and then pulled up on the rod, drawing my fish closer. I repeated. And repeated. And repeated. The night didn't get any lighter, and the voices around me crept in. Rebecca yelled from atop her long legs. Dusty took pictures. Even Gary began to cheer.

The pivotal moment in any tarpon fight is never the end, when you get your fish to the boat. It's several heartbeats before that, when your tarpon jumps for the first time. All tarpon do this. It's their last attempt at a fight, or perhaps their final salute to grace. After you've pulled and reeled so much your arms melt into the night sky and your mind fixates only on relief, the tarpon on the end of your line leaps from the darkness of the water into the stillness of the air, letting you know that you've won, that she's yours. And sometimes when this happens she seems to lock eyes with you. A line in the night from you to her.

And this is what happened to me that night. My fish jumped, and I felt for a moment a physical release on the line and a billowing inside of me. She was beautiful and airborne.

"Are you getting this?" Gary yelled. "Are you recording what this feels like?"

He wanted me to write a first-person story of my catch for the paper.

Yes, I thought. *There will be a record of this.*

"I caught a tremendous fish," Elizabeth Bishop writes when I peek into my dog-eared collection of her poetry from college. "And then I let him go," is how she ends that poem. Her fish was homely and battered, his worth in what he had escaped over many long years. And he did not fight.

My fish was young and bright and bigger than me. And her fight is why I remember her today. The other difference between me and Elizabeth Bishop is this: I didn't let my fish go. Not willingly. If I had been able to have it my way, I might have kept her. I might have hauled her in and hung her up on the dock for a picture with me like they did in the old days. I might have had her mounted and hung her above my living-room fireplace in whatever state or country where I would eventually settle, with whichever woman I would eventually be able to keep loving without feeling trapped.

The truth is I left my bass fisherwoman because she left me first. One night while she slept, I sat on our porch in the thick Florida air and kissed another girl who took pictures and talked about poetry, a girl who had graduated from college and who understood me—or the me I felt I was becoming then. Telling Penny the story of that kiss the next morning was the unfolding. She woke up and looked at me in such a soft way, such an ordinarily soft way, that for a moment I almost stopped myself. I knew her eyes would change when she heard. And they did.

"I'm sorry," I said after I was done confessing, but she turned her back to me and found a spot on our porch, casting her gaze back into the swamp behind our house without a word. I curled on the couch and watched her, registering the beginning of change.

A little tug gives way to a pull and then a yank, and soon the kite at the end of your unfurling line is a fish, and that pull is a fight you either lose or you don't. These things happen to everyone at least once. But then they happen to you, and you never forget them.

MY CHOICE

I WAS DRIVING to the newsroom when I saw the first billboard assuring me I could change. It was winter on the Gulf Coast of Texas, and the wetlands buffeting the highway sparkled every so often with the fall of another cast net capturing bait. Just beyond the McDonald's, with its line of drive-thru breakfast orders, was a giant photo of an adonic man smiling confidently beside the message, "I Questioned Homosexuality. Change is Possible. Discover How." I spotted another billboard, nearly identical to the first, once I reached Texas City's mini-metropolis of petrochemical plants. Only this time it was a smiling woman. Both listed a website called Love Won Out.

At my desk that morning, rather than sifting through e-mails or story assignments, I went to the billboard's web site. Love Won Out, I learned, was a conference that tours the country every year teaching "the truth that homosexuality is preventable and treatable."

I immediately wrote an e-mail to my editor in the main newsroom in Galveston and suggested a story.

"Wait," he responded.

Usually if the story was good, I never had to wait.

I wrote back, "Just because I am a lesbian doesn't mean I can't cover this story fairly and objectively."

He didn't respond. But later that day he gave me the go-ahead. People were already calling and e-mailing about the billboards, and most of them were livid. He told me to get something for that weekend and that we'd do another story about the conference once it came to town, and then he added, "I would equate it more with a black reporter covering the Klan. We've done that before, too. But we had to think about it first."

The difference, of course, was that a black reporter couldn't hide the color of her skin, but I could easily hide my sexuality. I was in my early twenties then. I had long, blonde hair and a tendency to smile even when I wasn't happy. People usually assumed I was straight, so acting the part just meant remembering not to say too much about myself.

When I called the number for Focus on the Family, I introduced myself as a reporter and was quickly connected to a squeaky-voiced spokesman named Christopher. He told me that the conference would be at a megachurch near Houston, that hundreds were expected to attend, and that many had been "saved" already.

"And the billboards?" I asked.

"Oh," he said. "Those weren't from us."

"They weren't?"

"Well, they're our design, but a local businessman funded them."

That businessman's name was B. Joe Cline, and he ran his own ex-gay ministry on Galveston Island. He had a son who had once identified as gay, Christopher said, and then he asked if I'd like to talk with the two of them.

"Yes, please," I said.

Act I

B. Joe arrived to our interview early carrying a box of dough-nuts and a plastic bag.

"Try one," he motioned to the doughnuts while taking a seat at the conference table in our newspaper's main office. When I took one, he looked pleased.

Over the phone B. Joe had sounded like a stew of stereo-types: used-car salesman, Baptist preacher, grandfather. Meet-ing him in person I realized how telling a voice can be. He wore a two-tone, mauve suit, and his thinning brown hair was held in place with what appeared to be hairspray. His eyebrows arched perfectly above sunken eyes, and his tanned face had begun to sag with age. When I asked how old he was, B. Joe told me he was sixty-one. Five years later another newspaper would list him as being seventy-five.

In the plastic bag I found two folders, a CD, a cassette tape, and a video, each detailing the "causes and cures of homosexu-ality." I put the bag down between us and asked B. Joe to tell me a little bit about himself while we waited for his son Lanny to arrive. Biography always puts me at ease.

"My name is Billie Joe—Billie like a girl's name," he began. "I grew up in Edmonson, which is an itty-bitty town outside Plainview. There were two hundred or so families there and not one of them was homosexual, at least not that we knew of. They just don't spawn them as much in the country."

I paused in my note-taking, but B. Joe didn't seem to notice. He talked about his dad, who had worked at a gas station, and about his wife, whom he met at a Baptist church. He told me about once paying fifty dollars to get his tonsils removed in a doctor's office, with only a local anesthetic. And then he told me about finding Christ and working his way from a part-time job at Sears to a corporate position at Merrill-Lynch.

"You know how I was able to rise so high?" he asked, his forehead glistening like a glazed doughnut.

I shook my head, but I had a feeling I knew what he was going to say.

"By being hungrier and more determined than the rest," he said.

"But there was a downside," he added, his voice lowering. "I wasn't there that much when Lanny was growing up. If I had to travel, I traveled, and that meant my youngest boy grew closer to his mother, too close we realize now, and I know that contributed to what happened later."

As if on cue, Lanny came around the corner. He told us he had been at the newspaper offices for at least ten minutes, but the receptionist couldn't find me, and so he had sat quietly up front, waiting. Eventually he had heard his father's voice and followed the sound to the conference room.

Unlike B. Joe, Lanny spoke in a quiet, measured tone. He was so skinny I could see his clavicle through his shirt. He had smooth skin, wore glasses, and sat and stood with a straight back. I offered him one of his father's doughnuts, but he declined.

Once he was settled into a seat, I asked him to tell me his story, too, but this time my question felt strange. The coming-out story is a trope in queer culture. We all have one. We tell them to new friends and new lovers. We share them at chance meetings or dinner parties. But I had never asked someone to tell me his coming-out-and-going-back-in story.

Lanny started, like most of us do, with his childhood. He shared familiar anecdotes about feeling different as a kid and having more girl friends than guy friends. In his twenties, he said, he moved to Colorado, and there he was even lonelier. He felt lost.

He paused, pressing his hands against his thighs, and looked up at me. His father and I both nodded.

"Then one day I saw this ad in a local newspaper for a gay and lesbian organization. So I just called them up, and the next thing you know I went to a meeting, and suddenly I felt like it all made sense. All those feelings of being different. It suddenly clicked that I was homosexual."

It was 1978. That same year Lanny came out to his parents in a letter.

"When we got that letter my wife threw herself on the bed and cried," B. Joe interrupted.

"And you?" I asked him.

B. Joe shook his head. "I waited, and then I sat down at my desk and wrote my son a love letter. I told him I loved him no matter what, but I didn't approve of what he was doing. I soaked that letter in my tears."

I looked at Lanny. He was taller than his father, but he seemed smaller in the conference-room chair. His shirt and pants were perfectly pressed. He reminded me of a bird.

"He was very accepting," he assured me. "I knew lots of people who had been completely rejected by their parents, and my mom and dad never did that."

Normally this is where a coming-out story ends. The acknowledgement of one's true identity is the final act of self-awakening that brings the narrative to a close.

But Lanny kept talking.

"Soon after that I started to get dissatisfied with the homosexual community," he explained. "I was still a Christian, and I wanted to love before I lusted, but it didn't seem like there was that sort of option out there for me. Much of the social life centered around bars, and pretty soon I started feeling just as alone and different in that world as I had being outside of it. I got pretty down, and I didn't know what to do."

What he did was move back to Galveston, back in with his parents. He got a job with his dad and began going to a local church. At some point, he said, he made the decision to change.

"Two years after I had come out to my parents," he said, "I told them I just couldn't do it anymore."

There was a silence in the room. This was meant to be the moment of resolution in Lanny's story, but I didn't feel closure.

"So do you consider yourself straight now?" I finally asked.

Lanny shook his head.

"I consider myself a struggler. I am content right now to make God my only romantic love."

At that point B. Joe excused himself to go to the bathroom. Lanny and I sat in silence for a moment, watching his father disappear.

"Do you ever stray?" I asked once his father was gone. It wasn't really a reporter's question. It was a personal one.

"Sometimes," he started. "When I am driving down the Seawall."

His voice trailed off there, but I understood what he meant. Galveston is lined for more than one hundred blocks by a massive seawall built to protect the island from hurricanes. But in the warm months its sharp concrete walls are softened by the wet, sweating bodies of joggers, sunbathers, and surfers. The seawall in those moments is less a barrier than a siren—at least if you are someone like Lanny, and you're trying not to look.

Act II

That weekend my profile of B. Joe and Lanny appeared in the newspaper. I had tried to be as objective as possible in writing it up, but readers got mad anyway. A pastor with a lesbian daughter wrote a letter to the editor criticizing the billboards and the conference. Another reader wrote that she was worried such public homophobia would have a negative effect on the island's annual Mardi Gras celebration, which, she speculated, must attract a lot of gays. Ex-gays wrote letters in support of the conference and ex-ex-gays wrote about how harmful conversion therapy is.

Lanny also wrote a letter: "Some of us who grew up with same-sex attractions are not comfortable with them and want to explore the possibility of change. I am sorry there are people who don't want me to have that choice."

Driving home from work that night, I put in the CD that B. Joe had given me. Normally I would listen to NPR or, if a deadline kept me late, I'd choose an album that blended well with the night—Bruce Springsteen's *Nebraska* was a favorite at the time, as was Lyle Lovett's *Pontiac*. But I couldn't stop thinking about Lanny. It was his story that I kept repeating in my head, but it was also his use of the word *choice*. I couldn't argue that he had the right to "explore the possibility of change," as he had phrased it, but even if change were possible I didn't understand why he would want to do that to himself.

But I also hadn't been raised to believe that being gay was wrong or to fear the possibility of hell. My dad was an atheist and my mom, while religious, mostly went to church to hear the choir sing. We went to a liberal Episcopal church in Missouri for years until we moved to Florida and switched to a Methodist one down the road. There I joined the youth group and even once went on a mission trip to Guatemala. But even in that brief moment of faith, I never learned to fear for my soul. I kept a journal addressed to God for a short time when I was eleven or twelve, and in it I sometimes talked about being a sinner, but my sins were always innocuous ones: I was mean to my sister, I lied to a friend. By the time I came out as a teenager, I had stopped going to church altogether. It no longer interested me. But I never felt bad about that decision; I never felt like a sinner.

And so, I thought that listening to B. Joe's CD might help me understand what it would have felt like if I had been born into Lanny's world instead of mine. The CD was called *Answering Key Questions about Homosexuality with John MacArthur*. MacArthur is a fundamentalist preacher who claims in his books and radio show to "unleash God's truth one verse at a time." On the CD cover was a picture of a balding, white-haired, broad-shouldered man—like an angry god in a tailored suit. But his speaking voice, as it filled my car, was not the fire and brimstone I had imagined. He sounded conversational, even avuncular. He opened by sharing an anecdote about his recent appearance on *Larry King Live* to debate same-sex marriage.

"So I turned to this homosexual actor sitting next to me—he writes for the *Gay Advocate*, and I had met him earlier, and his name is Chad. And I said, 'Well, I think Chad wants to get into the Kingdom of heaven, don't you, Chad?' And he said, 'Yeah, I do.' And that was great because then I explained to him how God shows grace to the homosexual."

The CD was ostensibly an interview, with another radio host occasionally asking MacArthur questions about his views on homosexuality, but it slowly became obvious that the format was performative. Slowly, too, MacArthur's tone began to change. The interviewer asked him what the Bible *actually* says about homosexuality, and MacArthur explained point-by-point, from Leviticus to Romans, how the Bible confirms that being gay is "not a normal sin," but a particularly perverse one, one that was once punishable by death and, in a theocratic society, still would be.

"And so the question might be asked, 'If we did what was right in America, what would happen to homosexuals?'" he said at one point. "And the answer is, they would be executed."

I drove past blocks of inactive construction, turned left at a stoplight, and then left again on to the feeder road alongside the interstate that would take me back home. MacArthur was explaining why it's impossible to be gay and Christian as I passed under another "Question Homosexuality" billboard, that same adonic ex-gay man looking down on me with pity, or maybe hope. MacArthur moved on to Armageddon as I picked up speed.

"When God abandons a nation, when God gives a nation up to its own choices, when, in a sense, he removes restraining grace, the first thing that happens is they become preoccupied with sexual sin."

His voice was booming now, and it filled my car as he explained why tolerance of gays and lesbians was not progress, but a sign that God was letting us damn ourselves. And suddenly it was as if there were no distance between him and me, between his world and mine. And I didn't like it. I didn't feel guilty or damned, but I did feel shamed somehow, or maybe just sad knowing that so many people—all the people who listened to MacArthur and all the people who would be at the Love Won Out conference in a couple weeks—see the growing acceptance of people like me as a sign of the coming end.

I pulled up beside my apartment just as MacArthur's voice was beginning to soften. He said he wanted gay and lesbian listeners out there to know that there is still hope, that we can change if we want to, that we can choose to be set free. But I turned him off before he could tell me how.

Act III

The Love Won Out conference ran all day Saturday in a mammoth Christian church that, from a distance, looked like a giant strawberry cupcake. On the sidewalk outside a Lexus dealership next door, a small group of protestors had formed. They held up "My Goddess Loves Me the Way I Am" posters and waved rainbow flags as I walked past them toward the church door. A Galveston city employee I knew from covering government affairs stopped me. She was part of the protest crowd, and she said she wanted to give me a quote.

"As a lesbian," she started, and I knew she was outing herself, and she wanted me to out her, too, in the paper the next day. I wrote down what she said about being proud of who she was, and I tried not to envy her freedom to speak her mind as I walked away.

Inside the church a tall, freckle-faced woman in her twenties greeted me with a smile that hurt my cheeks.

"Did you talk to any of those gay activists outside?" she asked when I told her I was a reporter. I said that I had, and her eyes got even wider.

"Are they really angry?" she asked.

When I said they weren't her disappointment was evident, but she smiled anyway and led me to the front desk where we found Christopher, my media contact, who also looked like he had sounded over the phone. He was a mousy kid with light-reddish hair and a nervous energy most obvious when he made eye contact. He helped me register and then directed me to a seat in the back row of the sanctuary.

"The rules are, no approaching an attendee for an interview without first getting our permission," he told me. "And your photographer, when he gets here, can only take pictures of the backs of people's heads. We really, really don't want any one who comes here to get help to be identified in the newspaper, you understand."

I nodded. Of course I understood.

Looking around the sanctuary, I counted close to three hundred people, but Christopher assured me that at least nine hundred had registered. They sat in small groups or family units, though more often than not they sat alone. Our pews faced a large stage lined with fake potted plants and bookended by two large video screens, which would be used during testimonials to display childhood pictures of the speaker, and also during the "What Our Kids Are Watching on TV" seminar to show short clips of gay characters from TV dramas like *Law & Order* and *ER*.

I arrived in time to hear the tail end of a seminar titled "The Roots of Homosexuality," and afterward I stayed for the first testimonial. It was with Mike Haley, the adonic man from the billboards, who in person also had short-cropped, blond hair and a build that was muscular without being overbearing. He stood on the stage with a microphone and walked back and forth as he talked.

"We hear the message so often of the men and women who have left drugs or alcohol, but we don't often enough hear the powerful stories of those who left homosexuality," he began, as heads in the audience nodded. "We need to talk about this."

He told us about being abused by an older man when he was a young boy, about dating other men in high school, and then about becoming part of the gay community in his early twenties. In many ways his story was similar to Lanny's. He said that he had felt a sense of "coming home" when he first found other gays and lesbians. But then, after illusive searches for love and companionship, that feeling of belonging soon turned to isolation, loneliness, and depression. Seeking solace,

Mike found religion and eventually made the decision to stop being gay. He is married now, and he and his wife have two kids.

"I was always trying to be happy," he said in conclusion. "But I never was until now."

I looked around for Lanny, but I didn't see him anywhere in the audience. I wondered if he would call himself happy. I wondered how many of us actually are.

I eventually found him outside of the makeshift bookstore, where a three-for-one shrink-wrapped collection called "How to Love a Homosexual" was the best-selling item of the day. He was sitting with his father beside a booth for B. Joe's organization, Lighthouse Freedom Ministry, and they had copies of the profile I had written about them on display.

I tried to say something to Lanny, but B. Joe interrupted when he saw me.

"I want to introduce you to someone," he said.

He motioned to a tall man and a woman clutching her purse. They looked like a farming couple, healthy yet ever ready for the next crop disaster.

"This man was just telling me his story," B. Joe explained "He has a fifteen-year-old daughter who they caught with an older friend of hers."

The man began to tell me his story, and, as he did, his wife dabbed the corners of her eyes with Kleenex pulled from her purse.

"We immediately forbade her from ever seeing her friend again, and the next day we took her out of public school, the school they both attended," the man said, meeting my eye and holding it for just a little too long. "Now we're paying for her to go to the Christian academy closest to us, but it's expensive, so I don't know how much longer we'll be able to afford that."

"And she wanted to come here today?" I asked.

The man shook his head.

"She didn't know. We woke her up early this morning and told her we were taking her somewhere important. She's in one of the sessions right now."

The man said he worried that he only had two and a half more years with his daughter. After that she would be eighteen and could live as she wished, make whatever choices she wanted.

The wife dabbed her eyes again, and I remembered myself at fifteen. My first time was with my best friend. We camped out in a tent in her backyard, and, while her parents slept inside, we took off our clothes. We kissed. We practiced doing with each other what her boyfriend had done with her several weeks earlier. First her, then me. It was far from romantic. We were laughing and negotiating. But it was fun, and neither of us was worried about what would happen if we got caught. At that point neither of us even thought we were gay. I would later decide I was. But she never did. She met a nice guy, got married, and they just had a kid.

After I said good-bye to the couple, I looked for Lanny again, but he was nowhere to be found, and it was getting late. I knew I had time for only one more session if I wanted to get back to the newsroom and file my story by deadline, so I chose a slide-show presentation called "Straight Thinking on Gay Marriage," led by a PhD named Dick Carpenter. But within five minutes of the session, I realized my ability to be objective and fair had reached its limit. I was writing down what was being said, but I had begun to bracket the speaker's quotes in my notebook, as if to more clearly distinguish his words from my own scribbled thoughts.

"Homosexuals are getting more crafty, inserting so-called

tolerance education into the public classrooms, ladies and gentlemen," Carpenter said from the front of the dark room. "There are children's books in school libraries now with titles like *Heather Has Two Mommies.*"

Audience gasps, I wrote in a clearly demarcated section.

"Fidelity will go right out the window if gay marriage becomes the law of the land. What's next after that? Polygamous marriage? What if a father wants to marry his fourteen-year-old daughter? Who is to say he can't? Isn't that discrimination?"

No! I wrote.

When Carpenter moved to the next slide, I left the room, and a minute later I was pushing through the double glass doors of the church and back into the sunlight. I thought of Lanny, still inside beside his well-intentioned father, following his voice from room to room, and I thought of the fifteen-year-old farm girl I never got to meet, and I wished I didn't have to leave them behind.

Outside I found the people they so easily could have been. The protesters from the Lexus lot had dispersed, but in their place a new and younger group of queers and queer supporters, all dressed in rainbow colors, had set up on an easement between the church lot and the highway. They told me they had driven down from Houston for a "party protest," and as I took out my notebook, two teenage girls ran toward me, flushed.

"You know what we just did?" they asked.

I shook my head and smiled.

"We infiltrated the conference," said the taller of the two, a girl with Snow White features. "I got approved to work as a volunteer and so did she, and then, just now, during one of the testimonies in the sanctuary, we ran up to the main stage and started kissing."

"Yeah," sighed the second girl. "We had a sort of secret

signal, and when she made it we both knew it was time. We kissed for like nearly a minute before they knew what to do."

The Snow White girl smiled, and I smiled, too. She couldn't have been that much older than the daughter of the farmer I had just interviewed or than I had been that summer in my best friend's backyard. I took down her quote and walked back to the car, already constructing in my head the story I would write for the next day's paper. I would let B. Joe and Mike Haley and the Farmer have their say, I decided, but the story was going to end with those girls and that kiss. That was my choice.

MY HANDS

When you hold out your hand and the whole world stops
and you find yourself looking at the back of your hand,
which, the longer you look at it, looks starved.

—COLE SWENSEN

I AM IN a theater. Illuminated by stage light, the graying novelist leans into the podium as she reads, rocking the audience back in time, across the Midwest to a little house in a nothing town where a family plays checkers. In one of the back rows, I lean into the plush chair, holding one hand to my side and out into the aisle as I peel back the loose skin once rooted at the bed of my thumbnail.

My mind wanders. I am rapt. My index and middle finger dig, pull, and tear at my thumb. The author flips the page and turns to the subject of home—what it means, how it morphs and eludes us—and I abruptly recall the world around me, the rows seated behind me, the people everywhere who could be watching me. This, not the pain, stills me—though hardly in time. By the end of that night, as hands meet each other in applause, my thumb gleams soft pink, a throbbing corona of what looks like stretch marks around the nail's edge.

The first comprehensive analysis of the human hand also came as a proof of God. On his deathbed in 1823, Francis Henry Egerton, the Earl of Bridgewater, commissioned a body of work meant to prove that the universe came with a celestial design. In life the bachelor earl was a careless, jovial man known for hosting canine dress-up dinner parties and insisting on a different pair of shoes each day. But in death the Earl wanted to leave a legacy of teleological proof. One such proof was a tome devoted solely to the human hand. It was titled *The Fourth Bridgewater Treatises: Power, Wisdom and Goodness of God as Manifest in the Creation. The Hand: Its Mechanism and Vital Endowments, as Evincing Design*, and its commissioned author, Sir Charles Bell, produced 428 pages of analysis, methodically leading the reader through the curve of the human shoulder to the tips of the fingers, all the while comparing the shape and utility of these parts to similar structures in elephants, sloths, camels, and cows.

"It is in the human hand," he wrote, "that we perceive the consummation of all perfection, as an instrument. This superiority consists in its combination of strength, with variety, extent, and rapidity of motion; in the power of the thumb, the forms, relations, and sensibility of the fingers, which adapt it for holding, pulling, spinning, weaving, and constructing; properties which may be found separately in other animals, but are combined in the human hand."

Reading Bell's encomium to hands, you cannot help but pause every now and then to look down at your own. Those ten digits. These tiny tools. Hands are not only mechanically perfect, Bell argues, they also possess "the property of touch, by which [the hand] ministers to and improves every other sense."

But it is touch that does me in. If I only looked at my fingers,

I would never bite or tear at them again. It is when I am not thinking but feeling, when my fingers sweep check each other for loose or uneven skin, that I feel compelled to trim. I want to fix the errors of my skin, and so you might say that I, too, believe in the perfection of the human hand. The only problem is, I don't know where to stop. In the process of trimming, I inevitably leave a scrap of unevenness, some unruly piece of skin or nail that then forces me to return, readdressing the issue again and again. I am Sisyphus, and my hands are my boulder.

I had a lover once who would wince when she looked at my hands. We might be in the car, and she would glance over as I shifted from second to third, or we might be making dinner in her cumin-scented kitchen, me chopping carrots and her stirring lentils, when she would lean over to share some endearment and get distracted by the injuries lacing my fingertips. In these moments she would cover my habit from her eyes, her hands encasing mine.

With her, I tried for the first time to stop. I bought Band-Aids and cycled through packs of gum. She gave me organic ointments that rubbed fingertips to a shine and, when she spotted signs of healing, complimented my hands with a mother's pride. For a while this worked. I stopped biting and tearing in her presence, and when we took a road trip one June, the three weeks of abstaining allowed my fingers and fingertips to heal and my nails to grow thick and white tipped. I chose to see this as a personal triumph, an evolution of self, until months later when I moved across the country, broke off the relationship, and suddenly, almost without even noticing it, began attacking my hands again.

When I try to identify how all this began, I remember when I was seven or eight and my neighbor, a towheaded girl named Stevany, began to bite her nails. She nibbled at them with bravado for nearly a week before I finally asked what she was doing.

"Biting my nails."

"But why?"

"Because that's what people do."

Stevany was two years older than me. She and her older sister Dee taught me to play Spades and told me my first sex joke. In the winter they gave me their hand-me-down clothes, and in the spring they showed me how to drink sweet beads from the honeysuckle. After Stevany explained nail-biting, I spent days mulling over its potential, waiting until a moment when I was alone to try.

The initial bite came off, as I realized later, much like a first cigarette, everything unnatural but exciting, as if my body had a voice and that voice proclaimed, "This is not right" but then a whisper urged more convincingly, "Do it again."

And just like that a habit formed, then progressed. Until one day when I realized my biting was less habit than disorder. *Dermatophagia* is the technical word: skin eater. Another term for people like me is *wolf biter*, although no one in the medical literature explains why. Are fingers like wolves? Does biting and tearing flesh make me wolflike, make me wild?

The crux of it, for me at least, is this: I either see or, with my other fingers, feel a loose piece of skin dangling somewhere around the nail. I am then aware of this flap, and yet for some time I avoid it, avoid thinking about it, a challenge I meet with success until that moment when I fool myself into believing that I am acting subconsciously and then I pull, rip, tear. Skin removed from flesh. And what do I accomplish? Order. A sense of serenity. Satisfaction.

It's not the act of tearing or biting I crave beforehand, nor is it the pain afterward. What I want is the satisfaction of a desire filled. The forcing of errant parts of myself into submission. The belief that I am the maker of my own hands.

Another lover bit her hands even worse than me. A jet mechanic in the Air Force, she worked graveyard shifts, would drive to my bedroom at dawn, her uniform baked metallic, her fingers washed in grease that collected near nubs of nails where years of biting had inflamed the tips so much they splayed. After a shower her body would lower into the bed beside me, still smelling slightly of hot coins, the creases of her hands shaded bluish grey. Waking, I held her fingers against my palm, mesmerized by the brutality.

"Why do you do this?"

"Why do you?"

By comparison my hands gleamed porcelain, but she had a point. When our habits deform our bodies, we can't hide the proof of what we do. Still I wanted a distinction, a hierarchy of disorder. Even today I can see her in my mind, the way she would chew at her fingers with a determined cock of her head, a slight clench of her jaw. Her eyes always looked out in the distance, as if meditating on something no one else could see.

"Jenn," I scolded. "Stop."

And then her gnawing would cease for a few moments or hours, but at some point fingers always returned to mouth. This is a position of comfort for babies. It's a way of self-soothing, as well as a means of discovery. For the first few months, at least. After that, the idea is that our hands are known—discovered— and we should no longer need to put them in our mouth.

Our naming of the fingers is, perhaps aptly, wrapped up in the act of destroying them. King Aethelbert of Kent first listed names for the five fingers in the sixth century when devising a system to compensate his subjects for accidental amputations.

"If a thumb be struck off, twenty shillings," he declared. "If a thumb nail be off, let bot [sic] be made with three shillings. If the shooting finger be struck off, let bot be made with eight shillings." And on he went on from there: the middle finger worth four schillings, the "gold finger" six, and the "little finger" eleven.

Later, King Canute of Denmark developed a similar value system, but with different names for each finger. He, too, declared the most valuable the *pollex*, or thumb, and the least valuable the middle finger, which he called the *impudicus*. *Impudicus*, meaning "unchaste" or "immodest." The little finger, under Canute's rule, was called the *auricularis*, referring to the "ear," because, at least in some theories, that finger is the perfect size and shape to remove sticky wax from that part of the body. That finger later came to be called the *pinky*, it is said, because the pinky was once the name for a little boat in Scotland, the logic being, I guess, that pinkies are like little boats. Though what would this make the rest of the fingers? Tankers? Arks? Or, in some cases, pirate ships?

When I think about it, the desire began earlier than the biting. It started in second grade. One of my classmates wanted to teach me a magic trick. "Squeeze a blob here," he instructed, holding up the Elmer's and demonstrating on his palm. "Now let it dry."

We waited, waving our hands around in the air like acrobats.

"Now," he said, "You peel."

He pulled layers of dried glue off his palm in large snowflakes. I followed his lead, exalting in the illusion of skin removed from skin, in the tickly feeling it created. The rest of the day I tried the trick again and again in the back of the classroom, making and removing skin while everyone else glued Pluto and Mercury to pieces of starlit cardboard. Desire foregrounded the act. There was satisfaction in so succinctly removing a part of what seemed like myself without pain. The problem now is that it hurts.

Isaac Newton once said that, absent other proof, thumbs alone should be enough to convince us of the existence of God. Perhaps fittingly, the thumb is also an appendage whose evolution no one can quite explain.

In one of my favorite explanations, the thumb developed after the threat of giant rodents forced our primate ancestors into the trees. Opposable thumbs helped those evacuees clutch branches, swing among the canopy, and grab bundles of leaves for lunch. When we eventually grew tired of the arboreal life and landed back on the ground, our new thumbs allowed us to grip tools, wield weapons, and protect and feed our families and tribes. Our lives became less peripatetic, our tools more complicated, and our hands evolved with us: squat and square in early humanoids, longer and leaner in our parents and grandparents.

For most of these years, our hands were our most important tools; they were the weapons with which we battled the wild, the bowls and plates in which we cradled our meals. The phrase *living hand-to-mouth* originally characterized one major distinction between the rest of the animal kingdom and us. We don't bring our mouths to our food like dogs; we ferry the food to our mouths with our hands. Only recently has that phrase been equated with poverty. You live *hand-to-mouth* when you are barely surviving. Our hands are no longer tools: they are witnesses.

One day in the late 1960s, my mom decided to sign up for the Air Force Reserves. She was young with long, blonde hair, fingers stained yellow from nicotine, and nails bitten to the nub. A recent college graduate with experience as a chambermaid, she was directionless in that way many people are when they open the front door of a recruiting office. Vietnam was in full force then, so they should have embraced her, but something interfered. Fingernail-biting is a sign of a personality disorder, they told her sternly, and they turned her away.

Or so I remember the story. When I asked about it recently, though, my mom said she doesn't recall any of this. Perhaps trying to assuage me, she added, "I do remember a therapist I went to once when I lived in Boston. I told him that my fiancé was really pressuring me to stop biting my nails and I resented his implication that it was a sick habit. The therapist said, 'Well, it is a sick habit.' I never went back to him."

Another mom memory: I am very small and my mom asks me to help her weed between the bricks in our front walkway. "I need your tiny hands to get in the cracks," she says, and I look down, realizing that I do, in fact, have tiny hands and that, in this context, they are an asset. My hands are a tool.

Yet as adults we rarely contemplate our hands for longer than a few seconds. We look at them as we slip on rings, rub in lotion, grip a shovel, or hold someone else's hand in ours. But it is rare to just stare at them. I can remember only one time I did so. It was a dinner party, and everyone at the table started talking about tricks of the body. A young guy there, fresh faced, just out of college, halted the chatter simply by holding up his hands.

"I can't touch my thumbs to my pinkies," he said, modeling this disability, so odd that several of us protested.

"But wait!"

"No, of course you can."

"Just do this."

Suddenly we were all raising our palms up as if in prayer or praise, reproducing together the action he couldn't. We all stared at our hands then, thinking how easy it was for our little fingers to touch our thumbs, looking back at him with a tinge of pity, a hint of horror. In that moment, I swear we all felt gratitude. For our hands.

I pause in writing this to trim the nail of my index finger with my teeth. The noise sounds like the knocking of tree branches against windowpanes. I pull and chew until I bleed. My thumb throbs, and yet I can't stop thinking about another nub of loose, white skin protruding from a spot on my right pinkie that I tore at last night. I want to remove it, too. But I stop.

I am in seventh grade, and a girl named Brittany has everyone's attention.

"Did you hear she let a boy finger her during a movie in Mr. Adams's class?" Amber whispers in the locker room as we change from jeans to gym sweats.

I already know about Brittany. She's tall and has long, acorn-brown hair that never looks fully brushed. Her chest is round and matches the pendulum swing of her hips when she passes me in the open-air hallways in our Florida middle school. I know she comes from a poor neighborhood near our school and that she's mean, especially to other girls, which means she has never talked to me. Yet I can't stop thinking about her.

Fingering was a word we learned in sixth grade. But this is the first time a story has attached itself to the act. Hearing it makes me feel uncomfortable and strangely nervous, imagining a boy pushing his fingers into Brittany beneath the ambient light of a projector screen. Amber tells me the boy used two fingers, which also means something, I'm sure of it, though I don't know what—except that two is more than one but less than three.

What I didn't know then was that only a year later I too would go the way of Brittany. Those were the '90s. I permed my blonde hair and started wearing shorts that stopped far short of my knees. I met a boy named Shawn who told me I was sexy, which I decided was a compliment. I agreed to go to his friend Jason's house one day after school. And there, in a bathroom, Shawn touched me in the same way that that boy had touched Brittany in Mr. Adams's class. I didn't ask how many fingers. I didn't say a thing, in fact. Not even "This feels good," because it didn't. I felt gross, but also grown up.

Several years later I discover what it's like on the other side. Lesbians, many of us at least, make love predominantly with our hands. We eye each other's fingers—the strength of wrists, the muscularity of a thumb—with an unspoken foresight, as if divining an experience in bed through the curve and bend of an index finger, a middle finger, the strength of the *impudicus*. Of all lovers, then, we are the ones who should be most fastidious with our hands. I know this.

The woman I am dating now used to do palm readings. She tells me she has forgotten the details, so I try to refresh her memory with facts.

"The lifeline is the first formed in the womb," I say, holding her palm up for inspection. We are alone in my kitchen, miso soup reheating on the stove. "And then the destiny line. It's second."

She holds up my palms and inspects them, tracing these pathways, which on my hands ramble and digress but on hers run deep and uninterrupted from wrist toward thumb.

"In primates, the heart and head lines run as one," I say. "We are the only ones with lines that separate."

This fact seemed momentous to me when I read it a few days earlier. There is something special about us. Even without believing in God, I can see this. If it's not our bodies, then it's our ability to name them, to turn ordinary creases into metaphors and morph those metaphors into reasons to believe.

She holds both my hands now, and we look up, our fingers tracing each other's palms, only a slip of space between us. Closing my eyes, I can feel the spots on my fingers where the flesh is broken and raw.

"You know only the foot has more sweat glands than the hand," I say.

The soup has begun to boil, and its rumble soothes me.

"And at night the glands in the hand shut off. It's the only part of the body that does that—"

One of her hands leaves mine and traces the side of my face.

"—that goes to sleep."

There is no space between us now, and my eyes are closed, but I keep thinking about hands. What I don't tell her is this: babies develop nails in the womb as early as twelve weeks, and although this is thought to have an evolutionary benefit, it can also be dangerous. Some of us were born with a battlefield of scratch lines across our face.

In 1908 doctors characterized nail-biting and finger picking as a stigma of degeneration. In 1931 they called it an unresolved oedipal complex. In 1977 a team of researchers released a paper on the "Relationship of Nailbiting to Sociopathy," in which they determined that sociopaths are more likely than the sane to bite their nails. Only there was a hang-up. Biters have long been thought to suffer from acute nervousness, and psychopaths are considered to be the calmest folks around.

In recent years researchers have coined a new name for wolf biters, or at least for the action of biting: Body Focused Repetitive Behavior.

"Some have theorized that there may be the same out-of-control grooming mechanism in the brain that underlies them all," psychologist Fred Penzel wrote in a 1995 article on skin picking and severe nail-biting.

The most credible explanation to me, though, shows up only briefly in the world's first textbook on the subject, *Fingernail Biting: Theory, Research and Treatment*, by Norman H. Hadley. Forced stillness, especially in the context of the classroom, Hadley writes in his summary of popular theories of the time, is one explanation for why we do what we do to our hands.

"When we're forced to sit still, we have to reassure ourselves—play with our hair, scratch or rub our skin, bite our nails—provoke sensations that keep us aware of our body."

In other words, we bite our fingers because, in stillness, we have no other way of proving the reality of our flesh. To stop biting, then, we would need to find another way to remind ourselves that we exist.

I read an article once about people suffering from Lesch-Nyhan syndrome, a debilitating affliction in which the patients try, among other things, to gnaw off their own hands. Doctors now believe there is a self-destructive instinct in all of us that ordinarily is overridden by a stronger will to survive. Except in these people.

Perhaps by this same logic, wolf biters have survival instincts that are in overdrive. We want so badly to feel alive that we remove pieces of our own flesh, seeking proof. If this is true, then Newton would be wrong, and Sir Charles Bell only half-right. The hand doesn't prove God: it proves ourselves.

I took an art class recently, and the teacher told us, "You must be able to draw your own hand. This is where we all start."

Obedient, I stared at my hands. I saw skin peeling from fingertips, scars along the flesh edges. My ring finger bore a notch along its tip, a chasm in the fingerprint swirl that recalled beets chopped too quickly, a wound that had only healed a day at most when my teeth ripped it from its place. On my index finger was a rosy fissure, the remnants of a hangnail torn from its base along the seam of my fingernail. Each finger bore a similar scar, so that, at that moment, only my left pinky remained unscathed. I looked at all of this as if it weren't me, as a lover might look at me before she touches me. Then I began to draw, starting with my thumb and moving to my fingers, trying to copy the ridges and swells. And for that moment, at least, I was perfectly still, making a replica of myself.

MY Namesake

IN THE HOLY books of the Torah, drunks, whores, stutterer prophets, hardened pharaohs, masturbators, sinners who boil baby goats in their mothers' milk, greedy stepfathers, back-stabbing brothers, and slave drivers all bedevil God's newly grafted universe, but Sarah is the one who laughs at the Creator himself. She is ninety and barren and hiding in a tent when God tells her husband Abraham that his wife will soon give birth. Eavesdropping, Sarah "laughed to herself, saying, 'After I have grown old, and my husband has grown old, shall I have pleasure?'" That God eavesdrops on her eavesdropping and grows indignant at her laughter, or that she then denies having laughed, is less important than what happens next. The promised child is born and christened *Isaac*, which means "to laugh." *Sarah*, as any baby-name book will tell you, translates as "God's princess." They were together, then, a princess and her laugh, echoing.

I remember this story late one night when I cannot sleep. A woman sleeps next to me, and she turns into her shoulder, mumbling in echoes, "Ya, ya, ya." This word, a lazy "yes" in my mouth, holds twin meanings in Spanish. *Ya* refers to the present tense, as in "now," but with a change of context it can also signify the "already" of things past, as in, *Didn't that happen already?*

When my mom found out she was pregnant with me, she was thirty-one and skinnier than she'd ever been. The doctors had recently discovered that the source of her sickness, those bouts of vomiting, the headaches, and the monthly pain anchoring her gut against some tide unseen, was a disease called endometriosis. The blood that lines the uterus, normally thickening each month in preparation for a baby, becomes confused in women with endometriosis and crawls outward instead, coating the stomach, ovaries, and liver, as if they too might host a child. From such confusion women grow sick and lose weight, and often, as with my mom, the only cure is to remove parts of them. In 1977 the doctors who diagnosed her took out one of her ovaries and warned her that they might need the other one, too.

"If you could have a baby, that might heal you," they told her. "Alternately, you may never be able to conceive."

In that moment my mom must have regretted leaving her first husband; he was selfish and critical, yes, but handsome, brilliant, and ready, so long ago, to give her a child. My father was kind, but also chubby with an unkempt beard. He didn't remove his cowboy hat when he met my mom's mother in her Hyde Park brownstone. And though he wanted to marry her, he already had a son from his first marriage and wasn't so sure he wanted another.

Despite all this she said yes to him one night not long after her diagnosis. My father had picked her up at the airport, and, driving away from the tollbooth, he laughed at the rudeness of the gum-smacking, gaudy-lipsticked woman who had taken his money. My mom thought, *If I am going to raise a child, it should be with a man who finds joy in such small irritations.* But first she thought, *If I am going to have a child.* That I was born ten months after their honeymoon means she took on faith that she would love him even if she remained childless, but she didn't need to. I arrived twenty minutes past midnight on a cold night in January: her cure. After me, blood no longer grew where it shouldn't; with me, her barrenness filled.

In Hebrew the word for barren connotes emptiness, but also a life uprooted, as if the inability to have children also irrevocably cleaves you from the family tree. This pain is first seen with Sarah in *Genesis.* She is promised by God a child and yet remains empty. Desperate, she sends her female slave Hagar to sleep with Abraham in her stead, as if she could amend her body with the womb of another. The fact that Hagar then has a child named Ishmael, however, only enunciates Sarah's barrenness. She turns to her husband and says, "May the wrong done to me be on you! I gave my slave-girl to your embrace, and when she saw that she had conceived, she looked on me with contempt."

God watches this and yet waits thirteen more years before he cures Sarah. Then, when her son Isaac marries a beautiful woman named Rebekah, God repeats his trick. Rebekah is barren too until Isaac prays to God to cure his wife. Rebekah then gives birth to twins and names them Esau and Jacob. When Jacob grows up, he falls in love with a woman named Rachel, and she also cannot conceive. "Give me children, or I shall die," the barren Rachel screams at her husband. "Then God remembered Rachel, and God heeded her and opened her womb."

Biblical scholars say the stories of *Genesis* repeat in permutations, so much so that our minds have been primed by Adam for the generations of Noah, by Abraham for Isaac, and so on. Because Sarah is barren and cured by the Lord, we expect a similar pain and miracle for Rebekah and then Rachel. Abraham's famous trip up the mountain to sacrifice his son Isaac in God's name, likewise, echoes a trip into the wilderness made just one page earlier by Hagar with Ishmael. Cast out of the house by the suddenly fertile but still jealous Sarah, Hagar and her son wander toward certain death until God intervenes with not just water and food, but a promise to make Ishmael the father of a great nation. Isaac, it then follows, has little to fear when Abraham lays his body atop an altar of wood and slowly pulls out a knife.

In a literature class I took on the Bible in graduate school, the professor called such stories a genre of repetition, one seen with comparable pervasiveness only in Shakespeare—"and not nearly as well," she added. Although it seems to me that our lives make such patterns daily. Were we only able to step outside ourselves to read our stories, we too might be primed for futures that will repeat the past.

The year I am born, *Sarah* is number six behind *Jennifer, Melissa, Amanda, Jessica,* and *Amy* in the list of the most popular names for new baby girls in the United States. *Sarah* takes fourth place twice in the early 1980s and is third once, in 1993, the year I smoke my first cigarette, pretend to be saved at a summer church camp, and decide that if I ever have a child I will name her Madison. This was before people began using geography as inspiration for names, and I considered my choice clever.

Now the favorite is *Sophia*—last popular in the Middle Ages—and *Madison* is number nine, while *Sarah* barely hangs on at forty-three. Still there are so many of us. An online site that tracks "how many of me" estimates, conservatively I think, that more than a million Sarahs or Saras are living in the United States today. That is more than the population of Montana; it is the attendance of four Lollapalooza tours back-to-back. It is too many Sarahs to place emphasis on an original Sarah, and yet I do.

Sarah was also known as the Mother of Israel, matriarch of the chosen ones. In her one reference in the New Testament, she is simply called Abraham's wife, a symbol of the faithful spouse.

The story of her wifehood also repeats. In the first telling, it begins with a famine, with Abraham scared and Sarah too beautiful for words. God has sent them from their home, and they travel, starving and building altars at each stop. Outside Egypt Abraham turns to his beautiful, barren wife and says, "I know well that you are a woman beautiful in appearance; and when the Egyptians see you, they will say, 'This is his wife,' then they will kill me, but they will let you live. Say you are my sister, so that it may go well with me because of you, and that my life may be spared on your account."

That Sarah agrees is never mentioned, except implicitly. She and her husband enter Egypt, and Pharaoh takes her as his wife, giving her "brother" a dowry of "sheep, oxen, male donkeys, male and female slaves, female donkeys, and camels" in exchange. To protect Sarah from Pharaoh, however, God nettles Egypt with plagues until she is released. After he does, Pharaoh turns in anger to Abraham, repeatedly asking him, "Why? Why did you lie?"

Abraham doesn't answer until this story repeats itself. This time Sarah is almost ninety, and she and her husband find themselves near the city of Gerar. Once there, Abraham again says that Sarah is his sister, and again Sarah is taken as some-one's wife—this time by King Abimelech. In response, the Lord "closed fast all the wombs" of the house of Abimelech, healing them only when Sarah was returned to Abraham. Of course King Abimelech asks Abraham the same question Pharaoh had asked: "Why did you lie?" And this time Abraham responds, "Because I thought, *There is no fear of God at all in this place, and they will kill me because of my wife.*"

This much we knew, but he continues. "Besides, she is indeed my sister, the daughter of my father but not the daugh-ter of my mother; and she became my wife. And when God caused me to wander from my father's house, I said to her, 'This is the kindness you must do me: at every place to which we come, say of me, He is my brother.'" In other words, Abra-ham wasn't lying. Sarah was his sister, a truth we don't realize until the story repeats.

When I start thinking about patterns, I remember a day when I was no older than nine, likely still eight, and my mom told me about a friend of hers who ran out of eggs. That year I was just beginning to understand the process by which my body would one day produce and discard its flesh, month after month, which is to say that at that point any deviation from the tradi-tional script still confused me. What did she mean, *ran out of eggs?*

In the way I want to remember this scene, we were in our daisy-print kitchen in Columbia, Missouri, my mom at the table and me twirling into and out of the curling cord of our telephone. In those days I liked to wrap myself in the length of the phone's tail, and so I was entangled as my mom fed me stories of characters from her Chicago high school, of people she had known in college or through her first husband, all stories from that mysterious time in her life before I existed in this world. The name of the barren woman, we'll say, was Hagar.

"Then one day Hagar's period stopped," my mother told me. "She was only seventeen."

I stopped swirling and watched my sister out the window on the porch, swinging naked in the hammock. My older half brother was asleep in the basement. My father and younger brother were out, or gone, or too far away to interrupt.

"But why?" I asked.

"Turns out she only had eggs in one ovary. The other, completely empty."

My mom pointed then to the spots above her hips, spots where we must all have ovaries. "It meant she could never have kids."

At that moment she likely recalled her own infertility scare. I thought about my body, certain that Hagar was a warning, but for a danger I could not yet name.

Namesakes are tricky. Literally from the phrase *for the name's sake*, the term has been muddied by years of use. In some dictionaries a namesake applies to all people with a shared name, while in others it is reserved specifically for the name of the person whose name is taken by another. According to this second reading, Sarah would be my namesake. Yet in its original use, namesake referred not to the source of the name but to its reincarnation. I am then Sarah's namesake. It is for her sake that I have my name.

The woman I am sleeping with tells me that her green shoes are bad luck, and at first I assume she is speaking figuratively. Though they are suede the color of a golf course, and though they lace unnecessarily from toe to ankle, the shoes otherwise seem to augur very little. They came from Spain; I know this because she buys everything of importance—chocolate, ear plugs, green suede shoes—in Spain, but I only learn of their *mala suerte* the day after we have our first fight. It is more a misunderstanding than a fight, one exacerbated by having too many forms of communication. The details are likewise unimportant, except to say that when she told me her phone *se murió*, I took this to mean a permanent death and didn't try to call. She meant a death followed by a rebirth—the lifecycle of a cellphone battery—and waited too long for my call, got mad, etc. I got mad at her for being mad without real reason, and then we made up. Only the next day, she blamed her shoes.

"Seems to me I shouldn't wear them," she said

We were in her bed.

"You're serious?"

"Of course. Before it was the brown shoes, too, but not so much anymore."

"But—" I stopped myself.

I couldn't develop an argument against patterns built on green suede shoes. Also we were naked, and when you are naked in bed with someone it is easier to ask about the hidden power of everyday objects than to dispute the fallacies of superstitions. I turned over, ran a finger down her back, and asked why she still wore them, then, these bad luck shoes.

"To change the luck," she said. "Like with the brown shoes. If I have a good day on the day I wear bad luck shoes, their luck can change."

A fallen gray hair brings luck too, she said, but you must keep it with you once it falls, and only lose it accidentally, as is apt to happen eventually, after the pleasure of spotting a lucky fallen gray hair fades. She began to believe in these correlates, she told me, when she moved to London and was young and poor and barely spoke the language. Faced with the uncertainty of a day, she would invent ways to map randomness. Climbing on to the bus in the morning, she might decide, *If there are at least five people wearing red, it will be a good day.* Then on the days that this was true, it seemed as if luck was with her.

In ancient Greece and Rome, signs were seen as translations of truths spoken by gods. The arch of an eagle flying might mean an auspicious day for battle. The liver of a sacrificed sheep could tell the requestor if the woman who recently caught his eye would, indeed, make a good bride. And the riddles of the oracle of Apollo at Delphi could determine where a whole people should settle.

Delphi was said to rest atop the center of everything. Inside the temple, a woman known as the Pythia—maybe young and virginal, maybe an old maid—waited on a three-legged stool above a crevice that leaked a gas thought to be Apollo's breath, but that was more likely a mix of methane and ethylene. It produced sweet smells that may have contributed to the trance state of the Pythia as well as to her visions and her truthspeak. Breathing this in, her signs came in the form of riddles.

"How may I have children?" asked King Aegeus. "Do not open the spigot of the wineskin until you reach Athens," responded Pythia, speaking for Apollo. But the king could not make sense of the advice and so slept with the daughter of an innkeeper on his way back home to his wife. The "spigot" of his wineskin thus preemptively opened, he never sired a child. Such punishment always awaited those who refused to unravel the riddle, to heed the sign.

Late one night, driving home from the grocery store, I heard part of an interview with an expert on superstitions. He said that it is easier for the human brain to be superstitious than skeptical because we think in patterns. Patterns soothe us, and so finding patterns where they don't exist and believing that they mean something, that they portend, is instinctual. I don't necessarily believe this, but hearing the man speak about patterns reminded me of Sarah and Abraham and how, while reading their story in *Genesis* for my Bible-as-literature class, I felt sick when I realized they were also brother and sister.

In junior high my best friend was a girl named Kara who loved U2 and drew giant pictures of eyeballs with sunsets inside them. Because we hung so close so often, and because we were both blonde and our names rhymed, people called us *Skara*. She was the first one I told about my half brother.

When I told her, I told myself too, because I hadn't remembered the story before then. It was late summer and we were lying on Kara's bed, talking about nothing or maybe about sex, and in a moment I remembered everything: the black-and-white plaid couch we kept in the spare bedroom of our house in Missouri, the smell of teenage boy and Clorox, a sense of immobility. Nothing that shocking happened with my half brother—at least compared to the stories of sexual trauma that fill this world—but enough happened that something in my brain blocked it, turned it to white noise until I was nearly sixteen and lay on that bed beside Kara. The idea that my memories could be so thoroughly erased and then rediscovered years later disoriented Kara so much that she called my story a fantasy. I tried to believe she was right. Though what kind of girl would make up that she had been convinced again and again by her much older half brother to rub on top of him on a couch while her parents were out?

The winter I turned thirty-one, I made an appointment to see a gynecologist so liked by my friends that they recommended her, repeatedly. I was filling out a questionnaire in the examining room when she peeked in, hollering, "Are you still filling out that form or are you taking off your clothes?"

My laughter, I suppose, indicated that I was still dressed. A sign on the wall across from me read, "Birth control does NOT make you fat!" I stared at that, leaving the last line about hereditary diseases unfilled while I took off my clothes in heaps.

"So you quit smoking," the famous gynecologist said when she entered a few minutes later. "Good for you."

She sat on a stool across from me with one pudgy leg crossed over the other, gripping in a way that reminded me of sausage. I had quit smoking almost seven years before and didn't remember writing anything about that on her form. But she knew, so I must have. She tapped a pen to her clipboard while covering my drinking, eating, and exercise habits. I changed positions in my paper poncho, first leaning back on one hand, then crossing my legs and hunching forward. It never stops being unnerving, waiting nearly naked in a cold room for someone to touch you. Finally, I told her that I had been spotting between periods and that this worried me.

"Hmm," she pondered.

In 83 BC, when Cicero asked how to find great fame, the oracle of Delphi responded, "Make your own nature, not the advice of others, your guide in life."

"Hmm," she repeated. Some part of me hoped that she would tell me I was barren. Because fearing a pattern is scarier than accepting that one exists. The reasonable part of me assumed she would tell me I was fine.

"Do you know for how long?" she asked finally. I shook my head. Like my father, I've never been good at tracking dates. Like my mother, I—

"Well, timing makes a big difference," she said with confidence. She told me to start tracking my spotting; she said keeping a calendar would help, that this would be the only way we'd know whether a pattern exists or not.

In some readings of *Genesis*, Sarah is barren as a plot complication. Without her anguish the book might become an endless series of names begetting names begetting names, with God only interfering when he is disappointed, as with the generation of Noah. Because of Sarah we have a pause, and God gets a chance to make life again—slowly. That he only makes it after stopping it is a fault we forgive because his intervention impresses upon us the possibility of miracle.

And, unlike me, Sarah wasn't given my name at birth. She began life as Sarai, just as Abraham began as Abram. Before Isaac on the mountaintop, before Abraham's nephew Lot fled Gomorrah and his wife turned back, transforming into a pillar of salt, God came to Abram and offered him a covenant: he would be the fatherhood of a multitude of nations, and he was given a new name. "As for Sarai your wife," God added, "you shall not call her Sarai, but Sarah shall be her name. I will bless her, and moreover I will give you a son by her."

It is interesting language, godspeak. God first tells Abraham not to call his wife Sarai and then adds that her name shall be Sarah. In one sentence we see the twin powers of a name, both that of the name giver and that held by those of us who, through speaking, legitimatize the giver's name. And the significance here is clear: Sarai transformed into Sarah because she was able to have a child. My name, then, could also be about birth.

After I remembered the story of my half brother, I doubted it until I turned nineteen and he got married. At his backyard reception, over a keg of Sierra Nevada from which we both kept filling and refilling plastic cups, he or I brought it up, and he said he was so relieved. He said that we had been kids, fooling around, but that he felt bad. I nodded and said it was OK, but it wasn't.

If we were in *Genesis* this might feel less like a weight inside. In fact, at the point where Abraham tells Abimelech that Sarah is his sister *and* his wife, the footnote in my Bible explains, "Marriage with a half-sister was permitted in ancient times (2 Sam. 13:13) but later was forbidden (Lev. 18:9, 11; 20:17)." But then, the discomfort of this story for me isn't really about incest; it's about power, and the ability to decide, yes or no, for yourself. I told a psychologist once about what happened with my half brother and then asked her what to call it. She asked, "How old were you?" Eight or so, I said, though I could not remember specifically. "And how old was he?" About seventeen. "Yes," she said with an assured nod. "That was clearly abuse."

After we left my half brother's wedding reception, my family and I went to a late-night diner, and, drunk, I retold them the story that I then knew to be true. The waitress brought me napkins for my sobbing, and a couple of teenagers in the next booth stared. The next day when I woke brick headed and remembered the story of telling the story, I refused to speak of it to any of them again. And we never have.

That was ten years ago. The ground is frozen in Iowa, where I live now, and I am on a street corner talking to my mother. She tells me that in Florida it is muggy and she wants to plant a garden. I tell her that it is beginning to snow here, heavy flakes that fall rather than float.

"Why," I finally ask, "did you name me Sarah?" There is a pause as if she is thinking. In the distance I watch a mother holding the hand of her toddler, his wobbled walk like that of a tiny drunk beside her. I am no longer spotting between periods; it stopped soon after visiting the gynecologist, right before I began trying to track it in search of a pattern.

"I don't remember," she says and stops again. Her pause feels longer in the cold. The snow is falling heavier now, and the mother in the distance disappears behind a building, taking her toddler with her. I find shelter under an awning and wait.

"It was just a nice name. Sarah," she says finally, and despite myself I begin to laugh. And though she could never know why I am laughing, she laughs too.

MY Narrative Transformation

MANOLITO HAS A huge head. Its bald contours gleam when he turns from the TV or bends to check the large plastic watch on his skinny wrist. The watch is also large and bulbous, like a green miniature of the boy's head, and it does not tell time. It was a gift from a relative who felt sorry for Manolito, a replica of the magic watch worn by a scrawny, bug-eyed kid named Ben Tennyson. The Omnitrix, as the magic watch is called, allows its owner to transform into various alien forms and fight evil.

Manolito watches Ben's show, *Ben 10*, from his grandmother's dining room in Antigua, Guatemala, his chair pushed up close to a TV beside two glass doors that lead to an indoor garden. His large head tilts back to stare up at the screen, and at times he is so still it is as if the cartoon boy, in his bursts of motion and tinny chatter, is more real than the motionless one watching him.

That is until I interrupt him.

"*Hola,*" I wave from the doorway. Manolito turns in his chair and stares at me. I repeat myself, "*Hola.*" Manolito turns back to the screen and sighs. On the screen, Ben takes on the form of a bowed-back gorilla alien, narrowly escaping the deathblow of his enemy. When I try to say hello again, Manolito turns to stare at me and squints his eyes until they shoot tiny lasers in my direction. If we were in *Ben 10* right now, I'd be dead. There is an explosion on the screen, and we both turn to watch it. Manolito covers his ears with his hands, jumps from his chair, and runs out the glass doors, through the indoor garden, and into the darkness of his grandmother's bedroom. In the story he leaves behind, Ben is in fire-alien form, surfing back toward Earth on a wave of flames.

"He didn't always look like that," La Señora tells us at lunch that afternoon after Manolito has left. In the beginning, she says, her grandson was a normal baby, a squirmy fetus in his mother's womb, where for most of the nine months he had a twin. His sister was slightly smaller than him, but with big eyes that matched his own and tiny fingers that looked just like his on the day the twins were born, he alive and she dead. Afterward, La Señora says, no one in the family knew what to do with the little girl clothes they'd bought to match the little boy clothes they gave to Manolito.

The doctor had blamed genetics, but La Señora insisted it was soccer. On a Saturday her daughter's belly had begun to hurt, so much so that they called the doctor and told him something was wrong. But there was a big game that weekend, and the size of the game trumped the size of her problem. He told her it could wait until Tuesday. By the time Tuesday came around, though, La Señora's granddaughter was dead. Which means, she tells us, that Manolito spent the weekend of the soccer game inside his mother's womb beside his dead sister.

It is this tragedy that formed the seed that later sprouted the disease that gave Manolito his large, gleaming head.

"He has cancer of the blood," she concludes. "The chemotherapy made his head fat and stole his hair."

We nod as we chew, straining to understand. We are eating meat loaf with green beans and tortillas made by La Señora's maid, Teresa.

"Of the what?" one of us asks.

"Of blood," another translates, *sangre*.

There are three of us living with La Señora this summer. We are her foreign boarders. Every week we each pay seventy-five dollars for a tiny room of our own on the second floor with a door that locks and three meals a day, every day but Sunday. Megan, a chubby college student from Texas, and Elizabeth, a pale Iowa junior who normally spends her summers lifeguarding, are both in Guatemala on a church mission trip. I am not here on a church mission trip. I am here to learn Spanish.

The three of us only see each other at the table for meals, where we try to speak in Spanish, though often Megan and Elizabeth get tired halfway through and switch to English. In those moments La Señora eats her food without looking at anyone, as if she were suddenly alone in the room. Her real name is Aida Ramirez, but I've taken to calling her La Señora in my head because the name seems appropriate for a woman with her poise. But also because I am still at that stage in learning Spanish when certain words or phrases feel especially significant or poetic. I do not think about the fact that calling her *La Señora* is a lot like calling her *The Mrs*. I think about how dignified the name sounds when I repeat it alone to myself in my bedroom on the second floor. I think about the *ñ* and how speaking it feels like belly dancing.

La Señora once taught school to the indigenous workers at the macadamia nut farm down the road, but she retired years ago, separated from her husband, and began renting out rooms to foreigners. Though she has no specific routine except meals with her boarders and the rosary she says alone in her bedroom every afternoon at 5:20, La Señora still dresses each day as if she were about to take a trip to Guatemala City. She straps on heels and stylish black capri pants to complement a tight, wraparound blouse that vees just enough to show the slightest line between her breasts. She sprays her thinning hair into place and lacquers her lashes thick. She reminds us to take an umbrella whenever we leave the house, because in Antigua it could rain at any time. And she tells us how lucky we are to have rented from her, because in her house every bedroom comes with its own bathroom. I sometimes feel like I have known her for much longer than the two weeks I've been living here.

"Does he know about his twin?" I ask La Señora after Megan and Elizabeth have said good-night and I've stayed behind, drinking the tea La Señora gives me for my stomach. It's been twisted in knots for two days from the *pepusa* I bought from a street vendor near the yellowest of the colonial churches in Antigua. I did this even though La Señora warned me never to buy food on the street.

La Señora laughs at my question, shaking her head.

"Yes," she says. "He thinks he ate her."

I look up from my tea. "What?" I ask.

"He thinks he ate his twin," she tells me, and then she says good-night.

My room in La Señora's house has one window draped by yellowing lace curtains. It looks out on to the second-story hallway, where lines of laundry run from the ceiling to the stairwell. This house, I realized at some point, was once a hotel. There is a podium near the front door, and on the second floor patio furniture skirts a bar that is never used. And of course all the rooms come with their own bathroom.

My bed is a single, and beside it I have a lamp and a table where I keep my books and journal. Near the window is a small chest where I store my clothes and a box of cereal, until one day when the ants come for the cereal and I have to throw it out. Now I only eat when called to the table by La Señora or Teresa. The arrangement makes me feel small and dependent.

It was the same arrangement last summer when I lived in Guatemala—except that finding myself dependent then made me feel free. That was the summer after I turned thirty. I had spent the previous six years working as a journalist, sometimes sixty hours a week, a job in which I always felt I had to be in control. I knocked on families' doors after their teenage sons were killed in car accidents and interviewed other teenage sons facing murder charges. I accused a judge of colluding with public defense attorneys and the head of a state agency of accepting kickbacks from a major energy company. I witnessed the execution of a young man whose last words before dying were, "I'm alright. Make sure Mama knows, alright?" By the end of my twenties, I was tired. I quit my job in Houston and went to graduate school in Iowa, and only there did I begin to feel like I was thawing. The following summer I enrolled in a six-week Spanish immersion class in Guatemala. It was the first time I'd had a summer free since college, and I'd made a resolution to learn Spanish. It was one of a number of new goals I'd made for the new self I felt I was becoming.

When I arrived that first summer, I could remember only a handful of verbs from high school, and so for weeks it was like

I was four years old, or even two. I taped a note card with the word *puerta* on the door of my small bedroom. I taped *ventana* on the window and *ladrillo* to the brick walls. I took walks each afternoon down cobblestone streets to my Spanish class near the plaza and recited new vocabulary words in my head. There were cut mango carts in the streets and quetzal birds on the paper bills and waves of conversation that I understood in bursts. The dogs sleeping on the sidewalks looked like puddles before me, and the volcanoes rose up from the horizon like the heads of forgotten gods.

There was one volcano named Pacaya that you could pay a guide to help you climb, and, though I was scared to do it at first, eventually I did. The day I went we split up into small groups, each with our own guide, and hiked in a line through thick forest until we reached a dark hillside of ash layered with fog. Then, like penguins, we scrambled up the ash hillside until we reached the lava near the volcano's peak. We took pictures beside the liquid fire and shared bags of pastel-colored marshmallows, which we gored with sticks and roasted over the lava until they burned. It was an active volcano, but we all trusted that it would never go off, at least not while we were there. Guatemala was the most beautiful and stimulating place I had ever been. That summer, and especially that moment on top of the volcano, I was sure the country had changed me.

Back in La Señora's house I put down my journal and turn off the light beside my single bed in my room with its own bathroom. The yellow curtains in the window facing the hallway remind me Joan Didion and her first years in New York City. "All I ever did to that apartment was hang fifty yards of yellow theatrical silk across the bedroom windows," she writes, "because I had some idea that the gold light would make me feel better."

Her story ends, of course, with a realization that instead of feeling better she just keeps getting worse. The curtains get drenched and tangled by afternoon storms, and eventually she decides to leave New York for good.

Most days Manolito comes to visit his grandmother in the mornings, and usually I have left the house already, so I miss him. But one day we come down to the table for lunch and Manolito is there, in the same chair, facing the TV and watching *Ben 10* again, with his back to us. We take our seats at the table and wait for Teresa to bring the plates.

On the screen Ben is about to activate the Omnitrix. He flips the round cap of his watch to reveal its face. Inside, instead of numbers and hands, there is a circle of shapes that Ben dials through to find the alien form he wants to take. After he makes his choice we watch as the DNA of his body combines with the genetic material of the alien form he has chosen, a process that looks like crystallization on the screen, as if a spiraling magenta quartz had burst forth from Ben's wrist and grown tumor-like up his arm and shoulder, past his heart, and finally to his eyes, transforming human flesh to alien flesh in a flash. The image is both cheesy and beautiful.

"What's Ben doing now?" Elizabeth asks Manolito in Spanish, but he ignores her.

"How old are you, Manolito?" Megan tries a simpler question. Manolito fixes on the TV; Ben has attained his alien form now and is fighting another, presumably bad, alien. Somewhere just off screen Ben's grandfather waits for him—as he always does. In each episode Ben, his cousin Gwen, and their grandfather stop at a new place in what appears to be an unending summer road trip: Yellowstone, Fort Knox, Las Vegas. And in each episode aliens somehow find them, which means that Ben must once again pull out his watch, transform himself, and save everyone before they can continue down the road.

One of us asks another question about the show, and finally Manolito turns to face us. He holds up his Omnitrix watch. His head looms. His look is blank.

"Is it a magic watch?" Elizabeth asks.

Manolito blinks as if her voice has injured him. He then jumps up and out of the chair and runs the same path he followed before: through the indoor garden and into his grandmother's bedroom. I look at the empty chair he has left behind and imagine him huddled in the dark of that room, hiding from us, or hating us, or both.

Ben's high-pitched voice continues screeching in dubbed Spanish on the screen. Elizabeth and Megan talk about their mission-trip group, the movie they just watched on someone's laptop, and their plans to hike to the top of Pacaya soon. Then they complain about the weather again, how it's always raining here and how all their clothes are wet. I tell them about my Spanish teacher this year, who says that we foreigners snivel too much about stupid things like the weather and being sick.

"It's like you all want us to be your mother," she told me one day when I told her my stomach was still twisted in knots.

I look over toward the TV again and notice that Manolito has returned and is standing in the garden on the other side of the doors, his breath fogging up the glass. Megan and Elizabeth sense his movement, too, and look up to see him there, his tiny body and huge head framed by flowers and waves of waxy leaves behind him.

He looks like an alien.

He is sticking out his tongue.

"Ah! He's flirting," Elizabeth says.

Manolito pushes his face closer to the glass, thrusting his chest out, now more hero than alien. As he does this, Elizabeth begins to mimic him; she sticks out her tongue, too, and places her hands to the sides of her head like the flopping ears of a monkey. Manolito pauses to watch before becoming a monkey as well, shaking free of his hero form as he stretches his hands wider than hers, elephant ears sprouting from his large head. Elizabeth, in turn, mirrors his movements. He mirrors hers and then exaggerates them. We laugh, but Manolito only stares back at us, so serious and so intent.

"I can do this all day, buddy," Elizabeth yells in English. "I have a little brother."

At that moment the doorbell rings, and Manolito drops his hands and disappears from the garden, running toward the sound. The click of La Señora's heels follows him like a shadow.

"He starts chemotherapy again tomorrow," she explains when she returns to the table a few minutes later and tells us Manolito has gone home with his mom. We nod. One of us says we are sorry to hear that.

"He hates to be alone. It scares him," she adds.

Teresa carries out the spaghetti and tortillas, but La Señora gets up from her seat just as we are about to eat, and so we wait. She comes back carrying a box of photos. One is of Manolito when he was still a scrawny boy of about three or four, with an almost normal-size head and his chest puffed up proudly. He is not smiling for the camera but has the look of a child with limitless energy, as if at any moment he would dash off and out of the frame. La Señora passes the photo around our small circle, and we each stare into it, imagining an animated, healthy Manolito, the little boy he once was.

La Señora takes out another photo. It is a black-and-white head shot of a handsome man wearing a tie. He smiles softly with the look of someone who has just finished one task and is eager to start another.

"My son who died," she says and passes his image around, too. We stare at his face, but none of us asks how or why this handsome man died, and La Señora offers no explanation, just a sigh, which she releases after taking the photo back and placing it on top of Manolito's in the small wooden box that she always keeps by her side, she says, when she prays the rosary.

That night La Señora hands me a small packet with two large pills in it.

"They're from my pharmacist," she says. "For your stomach."

I'm on my way out to meet other foreigners at a bar called Café No Sé, so I take the pills while we stand there in the kitchen among the browning-banana smells and dim light. I say thank you and leave the house without my umbrella.

At the bar we drink Gallos and chat in Spanish until eventually one of us gets tired and we all lapse back into English, relieved. It is cool and the streets are lined with the tiny blinking lights of the few houses still awake. We talk about Texas and about languages and about all the reasons we are here in this country, where all of us believe we are lead actors in our own play.

At some point, while we're drinking and talking, the volcano Pacaya erupts—though we don't know that yet. It bursts fire into the sky twenty-five miles away, dumping ash over the countryside and raining it down on Guatemala City to the west. I only find this out when I return to La Señora's house later that night and pass her dark bedroom on the way to mine.

She opens her door in a long nightgown to tell me about the volcano.

"Ash is coming down like rain in the city," she says. "Leave your door unlocked in case we have to leave."

I nod and say, "*Si*," but La Señora hasn't finished.

"It's dangerous," she adds, and I nod again. La Señora looks past me and into the darkness of the hallway. Finally she asks if I pray.

My stomach has begun to grind against itself, a pain more acute than what I've felt this past week. I say that I don't and try to move toward my room, but La Señora keeps talking.

"He was killed because he wouldn't give up his car," she says.

The pain in my stomach grows, and I feel dizzy suddenly, but I steady myself with the wall, trying to listen.

"They had a gun," she says, "but he refused to give up his car. And they shot him."

It is so dark in the hallway that I can barely make out her eyes, so I stare at where I think they are and try to think of a response. I picture La Señora beside her bed every afternoon at 5:20, repeating her rosary. For this son. For Manolito. My stomach feels as if it's being pulled toward the floor.

"I don't know why he wouldn't give up the car," she says finally. And then she repeats herself. She speaks as much to my silence as she does to the shapes in the empty hallway behind me. I imagine her then, before her son was killed, before Manolito got sick, perhaps even before her husband left her, or she him. I can almost see her as the woman she once was, transformed by a refusal to let time pass.

When La Señora finally says goodnight and closes her bedroom door, I walk upstairs to my room and throw up in the toilet I share with no one. I have diarrhea and then rise to throw up in the bowl again. I strip off my clothes and lie naked on the tile, flushed. My heartbeat is audible and feels too fast. I find the instructions that came with the pills from La Señora's pharmacist and read them for the first time: *Never to be taken with alcohol.* It says this so clearly even I can read the warning in Spanish. I don't know why I didn't read the warning before. I want to call my mom, but I can't. I want to call for help, but I don't know whom to call. My breath is short and fast, and I feel a pulsing darkness rim my sight. I lie there as still as I can be, convinced I am about to die.

On a mountainside nearby, Pacaya continues to burn. Villagers have run or are still running from the lava with their clothes and plastic bags of papers and photos. A TV journalist is hit by flying rock. He later dies. In Guatemala City black ash falls from the sky all night—so much so that no one will be able to see the face of the moon tonight, and tomorrow the sun will shine through haze.

I close my eyes.

When La Señora first told us the story of Manolito, what I remembered was the tale of the hero twins from the *Popol Vuh,* the Maya creation myth, which I read after my first summer in Guatemala. In that story there are two twin boys living with their grandmother beside a garden of green corn surrounded by trees filled with monkeys. Their father has been killed by the gods of the underworld, and the twins are soon called down to face the gods as well.

The gods challenge the twins to a game of *pelota,* a Spanish word meaning "ball." And though the boys win that game, the gods kill them anyway. They burn the twins in a giant oven and throw their remains into an underground river. But the boys cannot die. They turn their ashen bodies into catfish and then back to boy form again. This work of transformation amazes the gods but also makes them jealous.

"Show us your magic," they demand. So the boys kill a dog and then bring it back to life. They burn a house and make it rise anew. One of them even slays the other and brings his brother back from the dead. The gods stare at all this in awe until finally they can't help themselves.

"Do it to us! Murder us!" they beg, leaning back in the thrones of their court, tongues wet with jealously.

"Very well," the twins say. And, doing as they are asked, they rip the gods' hearts from their chests. But at this act they stop, leaving the gods forever dead.

Afterward, the twins return to their father's burial site to try to save him just as they have saved themselves. They fasten their father's decapitated head onto his neck and twist what were once his arms and legs in to the sockets of his torso, rebuilding from parts the shape of his whole. But the form they create is only a simulacrum. Their father speaks, but his words are not true; he moves, but not with the movements of the living. And so the hero twins are forced to leave his body amid the dirt and footprints of the ball court, though not before promising him that all those who seek hope in the world will pray for him. And this was said to be the beginning of prayer.

Lying naked on the bathroom floor that night, I eventually fall asleep. When I wake the next morning to rooster crows and the sound of water running, I do not feel changed. I feel grateful to still be alive.

Though I don't know so this morning, I will never see Manolito again. I will stay with La Señora for another two weeks before finding a new room in a boarding house without a mother figure or three meals a day because, as I write home, I am tired of feeling so dependent and childlike. It no longer feels freeing.

I will keep hoping to see Manolito once more before moving out, but each time I'll just miss him.

"He was just here," La Señora will tell me.

Or, "I just got back from seeing him in the hospital for his chemotherapy; he's weak but doing OK."

The last time I see her, La Señora will say that Manolito is doing worse, but that they still have hope. I will want to ask about his Omnitrix watch, but I won't. I imagine, though, that if he is still alive today, he has it with him. We all want to believe we have the power to change. Just as we are all forever asking each other to believe our tales of having once been transformed by this or that, by him or her.

The intrigue of the *Popol Vuh* myth is not that the twins can transform and resurrect, but that there are limits to their power. They may transform themselves, yes, but they cannot bring back their own creator, their father. They cannot return to what once was. If you accept transformation as a fact, you must also accept its permanence.

This house was once a hotel; this country, a Maya kingdom. La Señora's son was once a man who drove a car alone down a road like any other man who is neither hero nor alien. Manolito once had a twin. And I was once a woman, much younger than I am now, who believed a country might change her in the span of a summer.

MY LANGUAGE

THE CALLER CLEARS his throat when Doctora Isabel asks about birth control. "The rhythm method," he finally responds. In the background I hear a crackled announcement on what sounds like a warehouse PA system followed by the caller coughing. Doctora Isabel interrupts. "The rhythm method is acceptable, but do you realize," she asks, "that with this, biologically, your wife most wants sex precisely at the times you can't have it?"

The voice doesn't answer; it isn't meant to. In his pause Doctora Isabel's advice uncoils. She explains fertility cycles and female sexuality; she repeats the tenants of the rhythm method. "Very few men have the ability to resist a wife who wants to have sex with him," she slows slightly. "Do you see what I mean?"

The man assures her that he does. I see him cupping the phone near the open door of a loading dock, plucking flecks of dirt from his nails as he nods, watching the clock and thinking about his wife and about how they got themselves into all of this. He is middle-aged, I can tell this much from his voice. I understand enough of their conversation, too, to know that he is an immigrant, that he has five children, and that his problem—the reason he is calling Doctora Isabel—is that he doesn't want to have any more. "How many years have you been married?" Doctora Isabel asks.

"Nine," he says.

"So five babies in nine years," she emphasizes, her advice now obvious.

I am jogging up a snowy hill in Iowa with my dog when I hear that call. Mornings like this are how I've come to listen to Doctora Isabel, "El Ángel de la Radio." She is the most well-known Spanish-speaking call-in advisor in the United States, "a Latina version of Dr. Laura, Dr. Ruth, Ann Landers and Dr. Spock," to quote her website. On Facebook—where Doctora Isabel poses with French-manicured nails and a frosted wave of hair—she has fourteen thousand fans. She reminds us to breathe, she tells us that "a head full of fear leaves no space for dreams," and she posts, in both English and Spanish, on such topics as "the love boomerang," food as medicine, happiness, erections, perfectionist children, angry teens, meditation, and sleep deprivation, all of which are also occasional topics on her radio program. On the radio, however, she only speaks in Spanish, and the subject is most often love.

I began listening to Doctora Isabel soon after I got back from a summer in Guatemala. I was thirty then and, before leaving, I had been dumped by a woman almost ten years younger than me, a woman who liked to climb trees, who left glitter in my sheets, and who I had liked because she didn't like commitment. The year before that I had moved to Iowa to study creative writing after quitting my job as a newspaper reporter. But that first semester I drank more than I wrote. I threw parties and went on road trips and could not manage to stay in a relationship. I woke up hungover and alone on New Year's Day and made two resolutions: to write more and to learn Spanish.

In Guatemala that summer I finally began to slow down. I went to sleep most nights by ten, and in the mornings I wrote and then went running. I ran past the juice salesman and the coffee farms, and sometimes I ran up the side of a mountain and stretched at the base of a huge cross that had been planted there many years before. In the afternoons I walked along cobblestone streets to a small school near the town's central park, where for four hours a day I practiced speaking in new verb tenses: the present, then the past, the future, the conditional, and finally the subjunctive.

I understood almost nothing at first, then I recognized a few words, and finally whole sentences that let loose into a paragraph, or if I was lucky, two. I lost five pounds from the heat and the exhilaration of not knowing so much. I flirted, vehemently and in basic Spanish, via e-mail with a woman from Spain who I'd met back in Iowa before leaving. I fell in love with the estranging rhythms of the language. When I returned to Iowa I missed the bewilderment of feeling like a child again, lost in a world of words I was learning one by one. So I went looking for ways to replicate what I had felt that summer, and that's how I found Doctora Isabel.

What I liked was the cycle of the advice show: questions follow answers, which follow more questions, the essential problem repeats and permutates until it culminates in an answer. It was a structure that allowed me to parse meaning through context. Before my run each morning, I would cue up another episode, clip my dog to his leash, and head out into the early light, Doctora Isabel's advice buzzing in my ears as I began to sweat.

"*Hola, hola, hola!*" she enthused from her Miami studio at the start of each show, and I followed along, bisecting hickory forests and grass fields, trying to imitate her accent. The callers would say they felt nervous, and Doctora Isabel always told them to breathe, advice that took the form of a command: "*Respira, cariño.*" She called those on the other end of the line "*mi amor,*" or "*mi hija,*" and as she spoke I recited translations in my head: darling, my love, my daughter. I could understand only select words—husband, scared, Houston, work, abuse—but from those clues I built stories. I told myself I was listening not for the advice but for the vocabulary lessons. And for a while that's what I believed.

A few days after I got back to Iowa, I called up the Spanish woman I had been flirting with via e-mail. Her name was Marta. She had smooth, tanned skin, green eyes, and a gray streak running through her brown hair. She spoke to me in Spanish because she knew I wanted to practice and, though my speech was halting and riddled with errors, she waited patiently for me to finish my thoughts, only occasionally correcting me or offering up a word.

On our first date we drove to see a movie in a nearby town and arrived early enough to take a walk. We talked about my time in Guatemala and her summer traveling through Chile. It was warm that evening, and we both wore sleeveless shirts. I asked her to teach me slang, and she laughed and said that *guay* means "cool" and that the phrase *echar un polvo* means "to fuck" or "to screw."

"I need to study more," I said at one point, using the verb *necesitar*, and Marta laughed again before correcting me.

"*Necesitar* is only for real needs, like water or sleep," she said. "*Tener que* is what you say for everything else."

I told her that was strange, having two words for need.

"Only because it's not your language," she said.

We passed a clapboard house fronted by an American flag, a small community garden, and then a cornfield. Every once in a while we wove close enough to each other in our walking that our bare arms touched.

Two days later we went swimming in a lake. Then we went for ice cream. That night I made popcorn, and we watched an early Pedro Almodóvar movie without subtitles that Marta had to pause every so often to explain. Afterward we sat on the ledge of her front porch drinking beer. Around midnight we slipped into English.

"I like the English word *ledge*," she said.

"I like the Spanish word *tiniebla*," I told her. It means both darkness and ignorance, but it had always sounded to me like the twinkling of stars.

At some point we stopped talking and the night grew hot and silent. As I followed Marta up the stairs to her bedroom, I thought about that phrase *echar un polvo*. Literally it means "to throw dust."

Listening to Doctora Isabel in those first few months as summer turned to autumn, I am unsure what I made up and what I actually heard. Some mornings I would finish my run and realize I hadn't understood any of the show. It had been all trees, pavement, and sky and me thinking about just one word. *Murciélago*, the only word in Spanish that uses all the vowels. It means "bat." Or *me pones*, what you say to someone if they turn you on.

But other times it was as if I fell into a rhythm while listening, and suddenly I thought I could understand perfectly each stranger's problem and also the advice of this equally strange woman, whom I had started to think of as a friend. In moments like that I didn't hear individual words but conversations. I was running within the language, and it felt like I had entered the weather itself.

One day the caller on Doctora Isabel's show was a boy from Guatemala, so I tried to listen extra closely. He sounded upset, and at first I was sure he had said he was gay. But then he said that his problem was that he had been caught with a naked teenage girl. The caller assured Doctora Isabel that nothing had happened, but he said the girl's family wanted him to marry her. Doctora Isabel asked if he had immigration documents, and the boy said no. At first I couldn't understand how having documents related to the naked girl and to the caller possibly, but increasingly not likely, being gay, and while trying to understand that I began thinking about Guatemala and then about Spanish and finally about Marta.

At some point I lost track of the advice Doctora Isabel had been giving to the boy, and for a minute or two there were only waves of foreign words while I ran within them. Doctora Isabel advising and the boy listening; she asking and he answering. I passed students grilling in the park. I ran by blooming asters.

After a while Doctora Isabel's speech slowed, as it almost always does before she comes around to her parting words of advice. She said something I couldn't understand in a voice that grew softer with each word, and then she paused. "*No te cases si no la amas,*" she concluded. "Don't marry her if you don't love her."

And just like that the session ended. The teenager thanked Doctora Isabel, and the next caller was crackling onto the line. Her words were essentially about the magnitude of commitment. And that was the first time I realized I was also listening to Doctora Isabel for her advice.

What I loved most about learning another language was how

the world seemed to double. I would stay up late some nights reading through phrase books, enchanted by the thousands of expressions in Spanish that made so little sense to me. *De tal palo, tal astilla* translates as "like father, like son" but literally means "from the stick, the splinter." *Tomar el pelo* means "to pull your leg" but actually translates as "to pull your hair." Why the stick instead of the father, the hair instead of the leg? Why throwing dust instead of getting in the sheets? Why two verbs to communicate a need?

One morning I woke in Marta's bed, and when she turned to me and said, "*Buenos días,*" with a slight smile, I remembered again how everything is gendered in Spanish, even the day and the night. Marta was naked beside me, and I watched the light from the window graze her shoulder. I thought for a moment that this might be something that would work. Until she asked me to stay.

"Do you want to get a coffee?" she asked, switching to English.

But I was already out of bed. I said I had to take the dog for a run, and she nodded like she understood. I had told her I wasn't one to jump into anything. She'd said she felt the same. I got dressed, kissed her one more time, and walked home to grab my iPod, put on another episode of Doctora Isabel, and head out for a run. Only briefly did I wonder if I should have stayed.

I've been a runner nearly all my life. I started running when I was six and we lived in Missouri and had a next-door neighbor whose dad wanted her to be a track star. Because I had nothing else to do and few other friends, I would go on training runs with her. We ran while her dad followed us on his bike, and sometimes we ran alone. We ran two miles, then four miles, then six. We began training for a kids' triathlon. We entered the state track-and-field meet, running the one- and two-mile races in our individual categories. I never won a race. I didn't like competition. What I liked was running itself.

We moved away from Missouri when I was ten, and after that I almost always ran alone. In Wisconsin, where we lived for a year, I ran through snow-covered blocks, layered in tights and baggy sweatpants my mom loaned me. In Florida, where we moved after that, I ran along sidewalks that lined swamps being turned into suburbs. I ran past dead armadillos and sinkholes and through thunderstorms as thick as curtains. In Texas, where I lived after college, I ran along the bayou and on bridges that passed under a latticework of interstates. I was running in a Houston neighborhood when I met my dog Finn. He was a street dog who followed me for a mile back to my house and then waited outside my door for an hour, even after I told him I couldn't have a dog. Eventually I opened the door and let him in.

I have always secretly felt that I might be happiest without someone to spend my time with. Before Marta, most of the women I dated complained that I needed too much time alone. They said I put up too many walls. They said I was always trying to leave, always thinking about moving away, never still. With Marta there were none of those complaints. But still I loved to be alone. I would wake in the morning in her bed and leave her sleeping to go for a run. That is when I felt the happiest: when I was alone but with the memory of just having been with her. It was a contradiction that I wanted to resolve, but I didn't understand how.

That fall Marta and I took our first road trip: to a park near the Iowa-Wisconsin border, where a trail leads over Indian mounds to a cliff that overlooks the Mississippi River. We'd packed egg salad, tomatoes, and a loaf of bread, and while we drove I put on an episode of Doctora Isabel.

"This is her," I said, because I'd already told Marta about Doctora Isabel and how she was helping improve my Spanish.

"Hmm," Marta said.

The first caller was a mother worried about the books her son had been reading. She thought they were devilish and that maybe he was doing drugs. Doctora Isabel asked if she could talk to the son, and after the mother put him on the phone, Doctora Isabel began lecturing him on air.

Marta turned it off mid-solution.

"She's Dr. Phil in Spanish," she told me.

"She's not that bad," I said.

"Yes," she nodded. "She is."

We passed cornfields and giant, white windmills. An arch of birds appeared in the sky. I thought about how in the ancient world advice took the form of signs, which were seen as translations of a message from the gods. The cooing of a dove, the flight of eagles, the entrails of sheep: each of these held answers to questions about war or love.

Marta turned on NPR and started talking in English about a girl she had known back in Spain who had once walked on a man's back and stomach but balked when he asked her to walk on his face. I laughed and watched the birds out the window. Only later did she explain that the story was about sexual desire. I had thought it was about boundaries.

The next day on my run, I returned to the moment in that episode where we'd left off, and I listened again. I wanted to know what would become of the boy, if the hardness in his voice would eventually abate, if his mother would begin to cry, if Doctora Isabel could solve the problem they'd put before her, if there would be a fight, if the son hated his mother, if he really did smoke pot, and if talking to him reminded Doctora Isabel of her earlier days teaching science in Miami, long before she had gone back to school for education and psychology degrees and started the show that made her famous.

What I discovered was that Marta was right. In that episode at least, Doctora Isabel was too simplistic. She did sound a bit like a Spanish Dr. Phil. But even knowing that, I kept listening. I had this feeling that I would someday discover something important through listening to her advice. I just wasn't quite sure what.

We are a "confessing animal," Foucault once wrote. "The confession became one of the West's most highly valued techniques for producing truth." But we are also a voyeuristic animal. As much as we confess as a form of truth-making, we also exult in watching others confess.

One day the woman calling into Doctora Isabel was crying. She sounded frightened and I understood that her husband beat her and that she had no one in this country she could turn to for help. But she was speaking so quietly, her words running one after the other, that at first I couldn't make out anything else. Doctora Isabel listened, waiting. Finally she interrupted. "You have to leave him," she told the woman. I understood her perfectly. She used the imperative: "*Repite conmigo,*" "Repeat after me," she said. Then she enunciated: "*Soy fuerte.*" The woman hesitated and, when she repeated Doctora Isabel's words, it was almost a whisper: "*Soy fuerte.*" "I am strong."

But Doctora Isabel wasn't having it. "Say it like you mean it," she commanded. "Say it louder."

The woman tried.

"No," Doctora Isabel prodded. "More."

The woman grew louder. "*Soy fuerte.*"

She was shaking, or at least her voice was, and I worried the pressure itself might be a form of abuse. But then the woman repeated the phrase even louder, her volume bringing a shuddered static to my earphones, and I began crying without even realizing I would, running across the imprints that wet autumn leaves had left on the sidewalk.

For Thanksgiving that year Marta invited me to spend the holiday with her in Pennsylvania. We drove out to a small town called Meadville to stay with friends of hers who worked at a university there. One of them was Mexican-American, and the first night she and Marta stayed up late talking while I sat silently between them, trying to keep up.

Listening to them was like cueing up episodes of Doctora Isabel. "I want _____ the dog _____," Marta said. "Yes! _____ with me _____ this summer," her friend answered. At some point the exhaustion of being left out for so long overwhelmed me. I excused myself, climbed up to the attic bedroom I was to share with Marta, and, again without realizing I would, started to cry. When Marta joined me later that night, I said, "You don't understand what it's like to be so lost for so long."

"I do," she said.

And of course she was right. In some ways she understood perfectly what I was feeling then. She had moved to England alone when she was in her early twenties. For the first few weeks she could only say small phrases and words, mostly "Work?"—which she said so many times she finally landed herself a job in a government cafeteria. She lived in London for a year, in France for another year, in Chile for two years, and then in China for three years before coming to the United

States. Only now, she said, ten years later, was she beginning to feel at home among so many foreign sounds.

"You have to enjoy the lack of control," Marta advised me once.

"I mostly do," I said. "Except for when I really don't."

The day before Thanksgiving we all took a trip to Pittsburgh to see the James Turrell exhibit at the Mattress Factory. In one of the most famous installations, you walk into a dark space and follow a ramp up to a chair. There you find yourself in complete darkness in a space the size of which you cannot guess or even comprehend. You are told to stay at least fifteen minutes and wait to see what will happen. Not everyone can or does, but I did.

What happens—or at least what happened to me—is that red floating shapes appear and begin to bob through the space around you. They are like the blotches that appear in your eyes when you close them, but they seem alive. Turrell once called the installation an experience "where the seeing that comes from 'out there' merges with the seeing that comes from 'in here.'"

In the Gestalt theory of language learning, everything we hear for the first time in a new language is an inkblot test. Each time we hear a new word, we hold it up against the light of our own system of speech. Sometimes the sounds we decide we have heard are real foreign words, and we identify them as such and pin them there, their wings stiff, within a sentence. But other times they keep flitting away from us even after we imagine we have them cupped in our hands. In those instances we turn them into the words we want them to be. This is called the factor of closure. We see a rush of dotted lines, and we want to close them together. We hear a stream of sounds, and we want to knead them into tight, fat bundles of words. A sentence. A story.

What the Turrell exhibit taught me, and what Marta was trying to tell me that night, is that you sometimes have to let go in order to gain mastery. It was amazing how much that exhibit reminded me of what it was like to learn Spanish, but also—if I'm going to draw further parallels here—how much both of them resemble the incertitude of falling in love.

For a few years I thought about calling Doctora Isabel with a problem of my own. When I went to Guatemala again for the summer and, after that, when I lived in Colombia for nine months and Marta and I tried to make it work long-distance. Or when, after we moved in together the year I got back, we began to fight over the smallest of things: the temperature of the house, who would do the dishes, when and where we'd go on vacation.

After a while I began to imagine calling Doctora Isabel with other, less classifiable problems: when my knees ached and I couldn't run and I felt much older than I was, when I woke up spitting fire and wanting nothing more than to drop everything and disappear into the horizon somewhere to the south, or when something awful happened in the world—the Newtown shooting, the bus rape in India—and I wanted to disentangle what this meant about us, about our violence. In other words, when I was seeking closure for something that wouldn't shut. Mostly, though, I thought about calling when I was trying to decide if this was the time to stop running away and settle down.

But in the end I never called. I had listened to so many problems and heard so many words of advice that I felt I knew what Doctora Isabel would tell me if I were to call. "Don't commit if you're not in love. Don't let others tell you how to have a family. Don't stay with someone who makes you feel weak. But do take risks. Do listen to the advice you keep telling yourself."

One evening several years after we met, Marta and I were walking to a friend's house a few blocks from ours for dinner. It was dusk or close to dusk, and again it was summer. We were talking about the possibility of having a baby, when suddenly I looked up and, on the edge of the sidewalk near the grass line, there was a bloody dove. It was so white that the darkness of the blood looked almost mythical.

I stared and was about to point it out when, in the next step, the bloody dove became a crumpled sheet of crepe paper streaked in tar. I felt both relief and profound loss. A part of me had wanted it to be a bloody dove. Just like a part of me had wanted to stay forever in that world of the half committed and partially understood, that liminal space where everything is what you make it, where answers can be found in the flight of birds or in the words of a woman on the radio advising you how to live your life in another language.

MY WIFE

IT WAS SWELTERING the day I unmarried Marta, and we weren't even together. I was with my little brother in a Penske truck, the flat haze of West Texas rising before us like the credits at the end of a movie. Marta was with our three-month-old daughter back in Iowa, where the weather was temperate. Highs were in the 70s, lows in the 50s, and Marta was still married to me. Don McLean was coming for a concert that weekend, and there were drink specials at our favorite restaurant. Our three-month-old baby cried for milk and slept and cried some more. A couple of days later Marta and the baby flew out to West Texas to join me in our new home next to a university where Marta and I both had jobs—and where we were no longer married to each other. This was 2013, four years after Iowa had made it legal for same-sex couples to marry but still two years before the Supreme Court would decide that marriages like ours should be legal everywhere, even in states like Texas that refused to acknowledge that our marriage existed.

It's hard to define when the act of unmarrying takes place. Were we unmarried as soon as I drove out of Iowa in that Penske truck and into Missouri, where same-sex marriage was not recognized? Or was it only official once Marta had joined me in Texas, where marriages like ours were outright banned? Or perhaps the real unmarrying occurred when we changed our mailing address with the post office, which would mean we were unmarried for a week without even realizing it.

Getting unmarried to someone is also quite different from divorcing them. There are no legal documents to sign. There are no lawyers or judges explaining the terms to you. There is just you and your once-wife and your still-legal baby in a one-story, orange brick house under the beaming sun of a West Texas neighborhood where you feel the same as you did before. Or at least almost the same: you are both aware a difference exits, and sometimes you can even feel it—that small but still significant shift.

Before, things looked something like this: We were two graduate students in our thirties living in an Iowa college town. We shared the top-floor apartment of a small, blue house with a Juliet balcony overlooking the backyard garden. On Saturdays we walked to the farmer's market to buy tomatoes, squash, fresh eggs, and ground lamb. Sometimes I made fried green tomatoes. Other days Marta made gazpacho.

Marta was writing her dissertation, and I was trying to write. We had very little money but very open schedules. Sometimes we fought. I claimed Marta interrupted too much, and she said I lost everything she let me borrow. Then we made up, poured ourselves a drink, watched a documentary on Netflix. At some point we decided we wanted to have a baby.

Marta found out she was pregnant in September, and we got

married that January. We were in love of course, but we married less for romantic reasons than for the practical sort of considerations that used to drive marriage. Marta was going to have a baby, and we wanted to make that baby legally mine in the quickest and easiest way possible. We wanted to be a family legally so that being a family from day to day was more manageable, less bureaucratic. Marriage is supposed to give you that assurance.

We held a small ceremony at her brother's house one Saturday before an altar made out of Christmas lights, tulle, and two-by-fours painted white. I wore a dress covered with lions that my dad had picked out. Marta was in red, and her pregnant belly bulged between us when we turned to kiss. That night we played the *Shotgun Lesbian Wedding* mix I had made on Spotify: "January Wedding" by the Avett Brothers, "Settle Down" by Kimbra, "Compartir" by Carla Morrison, the Eels's version of "Can't Help Falling in Love," and, of course, "Chapel of Love" by the Dixie Cups, which as a kid I had imagined was the quintessential wedding song. Afterward we went out for Italian and met up with our friends to celebrate at a local pub.

A few weeks later the county mailed us a copy of our marriage certificate. We were official—at least in Iowa. Three months after that our daughter was born. And a month later the Supreme Court threw out the Defense of Marriage Act. We were official again, but this time in the eyes of the federal government as well—though still not in states like Texas or Utah or Alabama. We could now pay federal taxes together. And I could sponsor Marta—who was in the United States on a student visa—to stay in the country after she graduated that summer.

Except that Marta had already accepted a job in West Texas, in part for that very reason. Under DOMA, our priority had been finding her a job so she could stay in the country with me and with our baby daughter after she graduated. After DOMA, we were still committed to the plans we'd made under the constraints of a different system. And so in August we moved to Lubbock, Texas, and got unmarried so that we could stay together as a family.

At first we had other worries. Our daughter began teething, and I discovered there was no *New York Times* home delivery anywhere in Lubbock. We couldn't seem to find a day care that didn't have *Jesus* or *Christ* in its name. There were entire blocks dominated by smoke shops and strip-mall churches. Forests were unheard of, and a lush lawn was a sin paid for by hours of gluttonous watering. For a little while we despaired. Lubbock had been declared the country's second most conservative city a few years before we moved there, and soon after our move it was named the country's most boring municipality. It was nothing like East Texas, where I'd previously lived for five years. It was nothing like anywhere I'd ever lived before.

But Marta and I are both resilient, and I can be a bit of a Pollyanna. We began to find charms in Lubbock: There is Prairie Dog Town. Buddy Holly is from there. There are corn mazes, summer musicals at a grass-lined amphitheater, and several breathtaking rock canyons nearby. . . . There is Prairie Dog Town.

One day we were pushing our daughter in her stroller in our neighborhood, and I leaned over to kiss Marta. It was breezy but sunny outside, and I suddenly felt giddy. A young college kid in a pickup pulled up to the stoplight and stared at us through his open window before making an L-shape with his thumb and forefinger.

"Is that an L for lesbians?" I asked Marta as I felt my earlier buoyancy deflate. "Or is he calling us losers?" Marta laughed in disbelief, thrilled to finally have more cultural knowledge than me.

"He's making the 'Guns Up' sign," she said, and I realized she was right. The slogan for the football team at our new university is "Guns Up," and the gesture used to show this is a finger pointed in the air, like a cowboy's pistol.

I was instantly relieved. I began to think that life here might not be unbearable after all. If the worst we would face were imaginary school pride pistols, we could surely make it work as an unmarried-married couple with a child in West Texas. At least for a few years.

But then one night I woke up from a nightmare that someone had thrown acid on my face because I was a lesbian. I realized that Marta and I rarely held hands in public anymore, and that sometimes when a man beside me in line at the Starbucks saw me alone with our daughter and made an offhand comment about my husband, I wouldn't correct him. Very little of this had anything to do with being unmarried—at least on the surface—but it also had everything to do with it.

What you tend to see in most arguments in favor of same-sex unions is a push to quantify marriage. Federal marriage includes 1,138 tangible benefits. So excluding same-sex couples from marriage means denying us all of those benefits. The same holds true at the state level, though no one had quantified the number of benefits same-sex couples in Texas were denied at that time. (Surprisingly, one was the ability to legally divorce. In several instances the Texas attorney general had intervened in divorce hearings for same-sex couples, arguing that a divorce would be legally impossible given that our marriages were fictional.)

Most often, when I try to explain what being unmarried is

like I mention health insurance. Marta's university job provided her with a decent insurance package, but I could not be on her insurance policy because her employer was a public university and the state of Texas prohibited state entities from recognizing our marriage. This was an economic inequality that most friends and coworkers could understand. When I told them about it, they usually shook their heads to show their empathy. "That's wrong," they said. "That's fucked up," they added just a little bit louder. But I always felt like they'd missed the point. Or that I'd misrepresented the situation.

Not being on Marta's insurance plan was fucked up and it was wrong, but it was far from the hardest part of being unmarried. Instead, what I obsessed over were the smaller moments of uncertainty that seemed to perforate our sense of who we were as a couple. Like one day in January, around the time of our first anniversary, when Marta and I went to apply for a membership at the university gym. Two undergraduates working at the counter showed us a list of options. I pointed to the married couple membership, even though I knew that if they granted us that option they would be breaking state law.

"She's my spouse," I declared perhaps a little too firmly. One of the undergrads hesitated a moment, but the other nodded and began processing our membership.

We saved forty dollars on the deal. Later, though, I felt guilty for being dishonest. I knew we should be paying for separate gym memberships according to state law, just like two separate people with no legal ties. Then I got mad at myself for feeling guilty. Then I just felt tired.

I was not one of those people who campaigned for marriage equality state by state. Instead, I was one of a small contingent of contrarians—some called us "radicals"—arguing that marriage should no longer be within the purview of the government. "It should be a civil institution," I told my more conservative liberal friends, "not something overseen by the government."

"But it's not," those friends argued back, and they had a point. We can have our ideals, but those ideals always push up against life's realities. And the reality is that marriage is a legal institution, and like all institutions it influences our lives, no matter how much we intellectually resist it.

After Marta and I got married in Iowa something in my thinking about marriage—and about us—shifted. The "we" that made up Marta and me felt stronger and less breakable. Suddenly we were official. We were two people who would be recognized as legally bound—as kin even—by city administrators, insurance collectors, and hospital employees.

It was a bit like turning sixteen and getting your license. You could drive before, but now you had permission to do so. Driving is suddenly a legal act. No matter how much I believed marriage shouldn't be under the purview of the state, I couldn't deny that having one state (and then the federal government) declare my marriage legal and then another state deem it illegal affected how I self-identified.

Perhaps more importantly, these competing laws influenced how others treated married couples like us. Marta told me that after marriage equality was passed in Spain, little old ladies and ardent Catholics slowly warmed to the idea of a man marrying a man or a woman marrying a woman because the state had done so first.

"One difference," she said, "is that now we have the language to talk about it."

But in Texas people still lacked fluency when it came to marriages like ours. We met lots of supportive and educated people, but we were also regularly called upon to be ambassadors for our kind in ways we never were in Iowa.

When Marta started at her job at the university, some of her new coworkers asked about her husband as soon as she mentioned having a child. When she said she had a wife, some of them laughed and apologized, but others grew quiet or looked confused. Once, I tried multiple times to explain to a woman at our daughter's swimming lessons that Marta was my partner, and each time she misheard me. "Your parker? Your barber?" I can't remember exactly what she thought I was saying, but I know that after repeating "partner" three times I got flustered and stopped trying to explain who Marta is to me.

This is not just about Texas, of course, or about being unmarried. But when you live in a place that would unmarry you, the people around you seem to be less aware of the possibility that you exist.

Once, at one of Marta's departmental parties, I was sitting by the fireplace talking to the wife of a professor while my daughter bounced on my knee. Marta disappeared into the kitchen just as an older woman was making a beeline in my direction, led by the department's chair.

"This is Marta's daughter," the department chair explained.

The older woman's eyes lit up, and then she looked at me with a kind smile. "How lucky you are to get to hold her," she said.

I was so surprised it took me a second to respond.

"She's mine, too," I finally said with a smile of my own. But the woman either didn't hear me or pretended she didn't, because after that she spoke only gibberish to my daughter. And then she wandered away to talk to someone else.

I thought about that exchange when we went back to Iowa to

visit some friends a year after moving to Texas. It was cool and rainy, weather out of character for Iowa in May, but we welcomed the change from Lubbock's dry heat. While we were there Marta's old department held a party for her and a few other PhD graduates from the past two years. It was a potluck. I balanced a plate of quinoa salad and empanadas on my knees while our daughter ate pieces of cut fruit. When Marta's dissertation director stood to give a short speech about all that Marta had accomplished, she also mentioned our daughter and me, just like she later mentioned the spouses and children of the other graduates from that year.

"In addition to a dissertation, Marta also acquired a wife and a child," her director told the small crowd, and a professor sitting next to me ribbed her. "I don't think 'acquired' is the right word," she joked. Everyone laughed. Not an uncomfortable laugh, but a shared laugh. Our marriage in that context, in that state, was not controversial. It was just a fact.

Texas has changed in this regard, as has the rest of the country. The Supreme Court decision in 2015 meant that Marta and I were finally legally married everywhere. And even before that things were starting to shift in Texas. A year after we moved there, a district court judge ruled that the state's same-sex marriage ban was unconstitutional—though he then put a stay on his decision while it was under appeal. In his written judgment, Judge Orlando Garcia wrote that "Texas's current marriage laws deny homosexual couples the right to marry, and in doing so, demean their dignity for no legitimate reason." The word *demean* has stuck with me. It seems about right. It is demeaning to be forcibly unmarried.

But for a short while in our country it was very easy to do. First, you looked for a new house in one of two dozen or so states that still insisted that marriage could only take place between a man and a woman. Then you signed a lease. You found day care for your child and chose a new vet for your aging Lab. You changed your address and went about trying to make friends. You settled in, began to say that your home was there. You tried to forget that you were living in a place where your family was seen as a threat. You joined the gym. You celebrated Thanksgiving there, and then Christmas, and then Memorial Day. And somewhere along the line you realized that you had become unmarried. No matter how married you may have felt some days, your unmarriage was a fact you could not escape. It doesn't make sense that so many of us were routinely unmarried when we crossed state lines. But it is a fact that six months after we were married, Marta and I got unmarried just by getting in a Penske truck and starting to drive.

MY POSSUM

AFTER THREE DAYS of not sleeping, at least not really, I take Finn with me after dinner to dump a bag of garbage out back. I'm not sleeping because we have a baby girl, and suddenly she's not sleeping. She wakes every night with an animal like fury, thrashing her body and refusing to be still. And after three days of this, Marta and I are both slightly addled. So, when I unlatch the door to the back alley, I do not at first believe what I see. A long tail like a beetroot. Fur that sinks near the chest. Tiny gnats orbiting open eyes. It does not seem possible that a possum could be as big as a dog or that it could have just died like that, right there where I need to walk. And for the briefest of moments, I am convinced that someone has left it there as a warning. But then Finn begins to sniff at the limp body, and I call him off, throw out our trash, and hurry back inside, yelling, "You'll never believe what decided to up and die in our backyard."

A friend of mine is going through a divorce, and we chat about it on the phone a day or two before I find the possum. She tells me it's gotten messy.

"He's crazy," she says. "Really crazy. Our friends think it might be the rat urine."

She pauses then, probably for dramatic effect, and adds, "Did I tell you we had rats in our walls?"

She had not told me. She lives in East Texas, and I live in West Texas, and where she lives, she says, wall rat infestations are not uncommon. Hers showed up right when she and her husband were trying to work things out. Or when she was, at least. But then the rats invaded the walls, and the whole house smelled like rat piss for weeks. Her husband said it was driving him crazy.

"Some people just can't stand the ammonia," she tells me. "It didn't bother me or the kids, but he couldn't take it. He moved out. It was his excuse to finally leave."

A team of rodent specialists came and removed the rats, rat nests, and rat piss and rebuilt my friend's walls, but even then her husband wouldn't move back in. He never moved back in. In a month they'll be divorced.

Rats, like possums, are unlikable animals, but it doesn't mean we can't feel for them. I was living in rural northern Florida, interning at a small lesbian publishing house over the summer, when it happened to me. The editors had sent me and another worker to their storage shed, which was really nothing more than an old barn, to get boxes of expired tax documents down from the rafters and haul them to the landfill. The boxes had been up on the rafters so long the rats had made nests out of them, and each time we pushed a box down, a nest of baby rats came flying with it, making a splat when it hit.

The dead baby rats were fishlike in their translucent small-ness. But it wasn't them I felt for. It was their mothers, who never fell with their babies. Instead, they scuttled away down the rafters, their plump bodies heaving like an accelerated heartbeat. My internship was unpaid. I had taken it to get pro-fessional experience. But that day, watching those rat mothers scurry away after their babies had fallen splat, that was the only experience I've kept with me some fifteen years later.

When I check on the dead possum later that night, it's still there. Still dead. So I ask Facebook what to do. Someone, a semifriend who knows more about dead possums than me, tells me I have to call animal control. I look up the number for animal control and see that it's now called animal services, and somehow that makes me feel hopeful. To serve is much kinder than to control.

And so, with hope, I call animal services the next morning, and the woman who answers the phone tells me she'll get someone out as soon as possible to take care of my possum. I think to correct her. I simply found the possum; it isn't mine. But I realize that it's more mine than anyone else's. It's me who found it, and it's my number the animal-services worker will call when he or she arrives and needs to locate the dead pos-sum and *take care of it*. That expression also gives me pause. How do you *take care of* a dead possum?

Several other sort-of-friends from Facebook answer my question about the possum with a joke. They tell me to keep my back door shut, to run, or to give the dead possum a cookie. They post a recipe for Southern Possum Stew and suggest bar-bequing it.

"I believe this is why sometimes women marry men," a les-bian friend comments, and I picture a broad-shouldered man with bulldozer hands picking up my possum and throwing it in the dumpster out back. This is the do-it-yourself way of taking care of a dead possum. But I have a wife, and neither of us has bulldozer hands. Even if we did, we're both too exhausted from not sleeping to do anything as constructive as *take care of* a possum.

A real friend of mine tells me about the time she tried to save a dying squirrel. Her story is prompted by my story of the dead possum. Dead animal stories are contagious like that.

"I went to the barn," she says, "and got out the horse salve to put on a mangled squirrel that the dogs had gotten ahold of."

But when she tried to doctor the injured squirrel, it clamped down on her finger with its tiny teeth. She still has a scar.

"Beady-eyed shithead," she adds.

This is the way you talk if you grow up somewhere where there's horse salve, as my friend did. She lived on a farm in Ohio and spent her summers playing with animals in the ditch that ran between her house and the farm-to-market road. If you're like me, though, and grew up in a college town in the Midwest and then later a coastal city in Florida, you will have had very few encounters with wild animals outside of a zoo. The only live birth you will have seen was your wife's when your daughter was born. And even that one will have left you feeling helpless.

At home we have a small library of animal picture books, and we read them to our daughter sometimes, taking turns making the sounds for each of the animals featured within. We *moo* and *baa* and *meow* and *cock-a-doodle-doo*. She claps for more. Her first word, if you can call an animal sound a word, was a *quack*. We quacked when we saw the picture of the duck, and eventually she quacked back.

But I've noticed, during these months of making so many animal noises, that some animals are not given a voice. The fox, for instance. When we get to that page in our book, I always make a puckered-up face and sort of yap, which makes my daughter laugh. The fish sound is also hard, but not impossible. We pop our lips, and soon our daughter started popping her lips back. "Look, she talks fish," we say.

But possums don't even get pictures in baby books. The animals we want babies to know about are monkeys, elephants, dogs, cats, lambs, ducks, lions, tigers, and bears. Sometimes ostriches, toucans, or eagles. Sometimes even skunks. But the only possum you ever see in a kids' book is one hanging upside down in a tree, which is something you never see in real life. And then of course there is the bigger question: Do possums even make a noise?

You can, of course, look up any animal sound on the Internet. I look up "possum noise" after checking again on my dead possum out back, and the Internet tells me that the possum has a low, throaty growl that it uses along with a hiss to protect itself. *Throaty* is a strangely sexual word. But there are videos online of the possum noise, and it's true the growl is guttural—you could call it *throaty*.

After watching the possum hiss and growl, I turn to other possum videos, ones with titles like "One Mean Possum" and "Possum versus Raccoon" and "Killer Dog Hunts Possum," but my favorites are the more lighthearted ones: "How to Catch a Cute Possum" and "Baby Possum Swimming and Playing Dead and More!" That last video shows a baby possum in someone's backyard pool trying to swim while several kids yell in the background.

"Baby Possum, hello! Where are you going Baby Possum?!" Their high-pitched enthusiasm for all things possum is telling. It means that our kids' books could include possums, just like they could also include rats and biting squirrels and maybe even divorce and sleeplessness and crying babies, if they wanted to. Possums may be ugly, but they're not unlikable, especially baby possums in swimming pools or baby possums playing dead on command.

The scientific name for "playing dead" is *tonic immobility*, and it doesn't only happen in possums. Sharks do it. And rabbits. A few snakes. Some animals decide to play dead, but the possum has no choice. Tonic immobility takes over whenever the possum is deeply frightened. If sufficiently scared, it can enter a coma state and stay there for hours. During this state, a foul-smelling, green mucus leaks from its anus to scare other animals away.

We humans can do it, too. Not the green mucus, but the playing dead. We talk a lot about fight or flight, but there is a third *f*: freeze. Most often you hear about it in cases of sudden violence. Victims of rape will recall feeling paralyzed and unable to act. Victims of sexual abuse, too.

For me, freezing is what happens in nightmares. There is someone stalking me, and I want to run, but my body freezes. I am stuck to a couch, and someone has come to kill me there. And just before I die, just before I'm murdered, I wake up. Unfrozen. Not dead and no longer playing that I might be. I blink back the contours of my bedroom until the familiarity of it calms me. Until somewhere in the night I again hear crying.

The one time I killed an animal it wasn't a possum or a rat or a squirrel, but a cat. I was seventeen and going to a coffee shop to meet someone I thought I was falling in love with (teenage love is the opposite of tonic immobility: you feel like every cell in your body is blinking wildly). I was driving from my parents' house in the suburbs toward a coffee shop in town, and the dark road was almost empty save what I thought was a single plastic bag tossing in the wind across the pavement that stretched out before me. The bag danced and billowed, and I thought about how tight my heart felt and wondered if this time we might brush hands or maybe even kiss, what that kiss would feel like, how our bodies would be flushed, and that is when I realized the bag was not a bag but a cat.

I had no time to swerve. It sounded like a knock—a soft, thick knock. My wheels lifted for a moment over its body before settling down on the solid, paved road again. The sound a dead cat makes. I will never forget that.

The poet Gerald Stern once wrote a poem about finding a dead possum, though he properly called it an opossum, being from Pennsylvania and not from the South or the Midwest, where we insist on dropping the o.

"When I got there the dead opossum looked like / an enormous baby sleeping on the road," he begins the poem, which has always seemed to me like a response to William Stafford's "Travelling through the Dark." In that poem the speaker finds not a possum but a dead pregnant doe in the road—her baby still living inside her—and with this discovery comes a decision. He knows that if he doesn't push the deer off the road and into the canyon below, another car might hit it, which could cause more death or, at least, destruction. But if he pushes the doe, he will kill the baby inside her. His "swerving," as he calls his hesitancy before he decides, is brief: in the end he pushes the doe and kills her baby, but in doing so he potentially saves a future, human life.

Stern, though, refuses to be noble in the face of death. He

moves his opossum off the road but, in doing so, he rejects the poet's instinct to "praise the beauty and the balance" of death as a part of life. Instead, he just feels miserable. And so, in comparison to Stafford's meditation on responsibility, Stern's poem feels like a defeat, and yet his is the one I return to most, perhaps because it refuses to say what is right when it comes to death, or to life.

When my daughter was born, we called her *la ardilla*, Spanish for squirrel, because of the small fluttery sounds she made when we held her in the hospital in the days after Marta's emergency C-section. Marta was wrapped in bandages then and had to get up every so often to change a giant pad into which she leaked what seemed like an endless stream of blood. The hospital-issued compression socks sighed, and the IV clicked like an old grandfather clock. When new doctors or nurses came to check on Marta or our daughter, they said, "I hear baby was breach!" And then they said, "What a turd!"

Though Marta now thinks differently, I found the birth experience traumatic. The operating room was cold, and her jaw trembled from the jolt of anesthesia. A curtain hung between her face and her belly, and when I peeked over as the doctors began to carve, one of the nurses scolded me. "You're not supposed to look," she said.

So I held Marta's eyes until we heard our daughter scream. Then the nurses wheeled our baby to the nursery in her heated box while my wife lay there, her belly open, throwing up into a plastic jug. And for a moment I remained between the two of them, unable to move.

That moment of swerving was not simple, nor was my eventual decision noble. In the end I left Marta and followed our baby, not because I loved her more—at that point she still seemed like a wild animal to me—but because she was the weaker, smaller one. We are taught to care for the vulnerable first.

I am heating up a bowl of white bean and bacon soup from the night before, and the soup is simmering when I realize the animal-services worker still hasn't called. So I go out back to check on my possum.

This time I leave Finn inside. I want to get a good look. I want to make sure there isn't something green oozing from my possum's anus and to double-check that those were in fact gnats around its eyes. What I really want, though, is to touch its chest and feel if it is still warm.

I open the door, thinking about the possibility of my possum. It is warm outside, and for a moment I don't feel as tired as I've been these past few days. When I reach the spot where my possum had been, there is nothing there, only grass and a few tuffs of white-gray hair.

I check the alleyway. There is a man throwing away bottles two dumpsters down, and I think to ask if he's seen a dead possum, but I don't. There are really only two possibilities.

One is that the animal-services worker has come already and found my possum on his own, without calling me, and taken care of it for me. And if that is the case, I am disappointed, maybe even sad. I realize only now that I had wanted to be there when my possum was taken way. I had wanted to take part in how its story ended.

The other possibility, however, is that my possum was never really dead. No matter how sure I had been. And this option makes me happy. I imagine him, sometime after breakfast but before lunch, blinking away the gnats with only slight confusion and, as if life were never a question, popping up on all fours in the same spot where he had once lain so still, and then sauntering off on his way, his beetroot tail swishing behind him.

The next day my daughter begins to sleep again. As if she had never scared us with her fits in the night. As if we had been sleeping soundly all along and had never stopped thinking clearly about what was real and what was exhaustion. These things pulse up against each other: life and death, beginnings and endings, what we call ours but is never really ours to begin with.

MY BALLAD FOR YOU

Hang down your head, Tom Dooley
Hang down your head and cry
Hang down your head, Tom Dooley
Poor boy, you're bound to die

YOU WERE CRYING from your car seat, and without thinking I began to sing you "Tom Dooley." This crying out of loneliness was a new thing. For the first few months you cried only for food, sleep, or if you were in pain. But recently you had begun to cry because you felt alone, or so we assumed. We were new parents then, we knew little about raising a baby girl, and everything we did was guesswork. Singing was always one of our best guesses. Marta sang you Spanish songs about cats on rooftops, and I sang you folksongs from my childhood. I'm not sure why I chose "Tom Dooley" that day, but I did. And it worked. As soon as my voice disappeared in the song's refrain, you stopped crying. I stopped singing, thinking you had fallen asleep, and you started crying again. I started singing again. You stopped. I could only remember the chorus then, so I fudged the verses. There was something about a mountain. And something else about Tennessee. And really it didn't matter, because what you loved was the refrain. The swing of it. The dips and peaks. Tom Dooley hanging his head down to cry. We pulled into an empty spot at the grocery store, and Marta put you in your stroller while I sang on, facing you now so I could see you react. You beamed. It was pure delight. For months after that "Tom Dooley" was the one sure way to calm you, no matter the circumstances, no matter the time of day, no matter the cause of your crying.

Only later did I realize Tom Dooley was a real person. His real name was Tom Dula, and he was born in 1845 in Wilkes County, North Carolina, in the mountain range part of the state, southeast of the Tennessee border. Dooley is a phonetic spelling. In that part of the country, Dula was pronounced Dooley. He was tall for the time, five-foot-nine or -ten, and handsome with dark features. His widowed mother owned four thousand acres of largely unfarmable land in the rocky foothills that looked down on what is known as Happy Valley. They farmed corn in the foothills, ate cowpeas and sweet potatoes, and drank coffee made from acorns or sassafras root. They brewed moonshine. But Tom almost never helped reap or sow. He drank and he slept with the local girls. Then, when he turned seventeen, he enlisted in the Confederate army and became his regiment's drummer. He fought and drummed for a year, spent another year as a prisoner of war, and then returned to Wilkes County, where he began sleeping with the local girls again, including one named Laura Foster.

After a week of singing you the "Tom Dooley" chorus on repeat, I found the rest of the lyrics online. There weren't many: three short verses that in 1958 made stars out of three West Coast boys called the Kingston Trio. This was fifty-five years before you were born, and ninety years after Tom Dula died. The single sold three million copies, so you weren't the only one to love the song. It started with a DJ in Salt Lake City who got a hold of the album and liked "Tom Dooley" so much he played it again and again on air. Soon his listeners were calling in to request it. So he told other DJs in Boston and Miami, and they did the same. Their listeners were as crazy for the folk ballad as were the kids in Salt Lake City. I think of them sometimes, our fellow fans, when I sing the song to you. What is it that we love about "Tom Dooley"? Is it the surprising dip in the refrain? Or maybe the astonishing violence in what, for me, have always been the hardest lyrics to sing: "I met her on the mountain / And there I took her life / I met her on the mountain / And stabbed her with my knife."

The *her* in those lines was a woman named Laura Foster. She had big teeth with a space between her two front ones. She lived alone with her father, whose horse she took to meet Tom Dula late one night in May of 1866. She told a washerwoman she saw on the road, a friend of hers, that Tom Dula was going to marry her. When they found her three months later, she was wearing two dresses, one store-bought and one handmade, with a broach pinned to her chest holding the layers of fabric together. Her legs were bent to fit a too-small grave. Her chest held a knife wound. Her body was so decomposed that her father could only identify her by her fine-tooth comb and recently mended shoes. I imagine him looking down in the North Carolina dirt and nodding slightly to indicate recognition: *That's her.*

I was thirty-four when you were born. Marta had just turned

thirty-seven. We were both finishing graduate school, and I worried your arrival would upset the quiet pattern our lives had fallen into. Marta worried there would be something wrong with you. And in a way, there was. You were breach, but no one realized that until Marta's water had already broken. Within an hour she was fully dilated, and the faces of the nurses and doctors began to strain. "There's little time," they said, pulling paper masks down to cover their mouths. They put Marta—and you—on a gurney and rolled you both into the coldest of rooms while I followed, asking questions no one would answer. I didn't think, *Now I'm going to be a mother.* I thought, *I hope our baby girl is all right.* Now I know such thoughts are one and the same.

There is a perspective switch in "Tom Dooley" that complicates its singing for me. We begin in third person, with me singing *to* Tom Dooley, telling him to hang down his head, then telling him to cry, and finally telling him he's bound to die. But as we shift into each verse, the voice switches from third to first person. And suddenly it is Tom Dooley singing his story from his perspective. And in turn, I sing to you as if I were Tom Dooley. I push you in your stroller through the empty streets of our neighborhood, the boughs bare from winter and gleaming against the clean blue sky, and sing a story of how *I* murdered Laura Foster, then tried—but failed—to escape, caught by a man named Colonel James Grayson. "This time tomorrow / Reckon where I'll be / If it hadn't a-been for Grayson / I'd a-been in Tennessee." I look down at you while I sing and you smile up at me so fiercely I can't stop. I would do anything to make you not cry.

How can I describe what it's like to listen to you cry? I could write a wail for pages, but you could easily skim over the sound I try to recreate. So try this: imagine you are tied to a beach chair in the sun at the pitch of summer in Florida and left there for days as the gulls circle overhead, the waves lap, and your skin fries. Or this: You are watching an animal be slaughtered. The animal is a calf, and you stare as it is hooked and hung upside down, as it yowls with the approach of the blade. You want to do something, but you cannot. So you sing.

After I have been singing "Tom Dooley" to you for a month or so, Marta suggests we change the lyrics. The violence is what worries her. So instead of the first verse, we try, "Met her on the mountain / There I made her my wife." And instead of, "Stabbed her with my knife," I sing, "Loved her all my life." But the shift sucks the drama from the song without improving the message. Because what bothers me is not the violence, but the narrative arc: the way Tom Dooley is a poor boy, and Laura Foster remains nameless. Marrying her off instead of killing her doesn't change that. Besides, "made her my wife" has one beat too many. The words cramp up, our meddling obvious. And so after a few tries, I switch back. Not that you notice the difference. The parts you like best are still the swing up on the words "hang down" and the slow descent that comes with "bound to die."

———

When I was a little girl, my mom also calmed me with an old song, "We Love You, Conrad," from the musical *Bye, Bye Birdie*. It was originally a show tune about how a town full of girls loved a visiting pop star named Conrad—who was modeled after Elvis—but my mom made it into a lullaby. Instead of singing to Conrad, she sang to me, and instead of singing in the collective, she made it individual. "I love you, Sarah / Oh, yes I do / I love you, Sarah / And I'll be true / When you're not with me / I'm blue / Oh, Sarah, I love you." It's still sappy, I know, but when you're as young as you are, what matters most is that someone is singing to you. The content is secondary. At least that's what I tell myself when I worry I shouldn't keep singing you the story of a "poor boy" who murdered his girlfriend.

If we had rewritten "Tom Dooley," of course, we wouldn't have been the first ones. The song is a ballad, and ballads began as anonymous poems that changed as they traveled and were told and retold, sang and resang. There were romantic ballads and tragic ballads, and then there was the murder ballad: the true crime of that era. "The Knoxville Girl" is a ballad adapted from an Irish story about a man who beat his girlfriend to death. "Pretty Polly" has roots in the tale of a British ship's carpenter who stabbed and then buried his lover after he realized she was pregnant. No one is sure who wrote the first ballad of Tom Dula. In some legends Tom wrote it about himself as he awaited trail. And in a way this would make sense. Because even in the earliest recorded versions of the ballad—though Laura Foster is mentioned by name and at times even called "Poor Laura"—Tom Dooley is always our focus, and it is his death, not Laura's, that we are prompted to grieve.

To fall back asleep some nights—after you have woken us with your crying, after we have given you milk and sang to you and put you back to bed—Marta watches crime shows. I used to tease her about this. Later I complained. But she says crime shows put her to sleep because they are rote. Their predictability is soothing, like a lullaby. Often they open with the body of a dead woman. She is usually white and young and sometimes she is blonde, though we only glimpse her for a moment. Sometimes she is bloodied. Sometimes we learn she was raped, and even if she wasn't raped, she is often naked. Her body is still enough to contain the mystery, and as viewers we are meant to hold her in our minds as that mystery unravels. She never speaks, but without her we know there would be no story to tell. And so we are grateful to her in the same moment that we dismiss her. We need her unknowability: we depend on her silence.

Murder ballads may not be fit lullabies, but lullabies usually aren't happy songs either, even if they are meant to rock you to sleep. A famous Gaelic lullaby sings of famine. The world's first recorded lullaby, from ancient Babylonia, warns the baby that she must stop crying or the demon woken by her screams will eat her up. Then there is "Rock-a-Bye Baby," which ends with the baby falling to her death when the bough breaks. The Spanish poet Federico García Lorca collected lullabies and, in a 1920 lecture, asked why we have "reserved the most potent songs of blood to lull [our] children to sleep." He concludes that lullabies are less about the baby than about the parent: singing a lullaby allows the mother to vent her sorrow and rage and fear at the same time that she puts her baby to sleep.

————

Before you were born I hoped you were a boy. It was easier for me to imagine raising a boy, and so I was disappointed when the ultrasound technician told us you were a girl, even though I tried not to be. Later, Marta needed another ultrasound, and I asked the technician to make sure you were really a girl. When she said yes, I gave up. You were small and red and screamed like a rattle when you were born, and I cried behind my paper face mask and glasses and kept touching your tiny, curled hand while the nurses scrubbed you clean under the heating lamp. In the days and weeks that followed, people came to see you. They gifted us pink things. They called you pretty. I hated them for that, but I accepted what they gave us without a word. Over time I softened to the idea. I could see advantages. But even now there are moments when I wish, without wanting to wish, that you weren't a girl. I wish this for you now more than I wish it for me. I know I need to stop. I was a girl once, and it hasn't ruined me. But it has made things harder.

In one book about the Tom Dula legend, an amateur historian writes that Laura Foster was "a young woman of shaded reputation" before adding later that "Tom Dula was a victim of civil and political conditions of his time." Another book calls Laura "raunchy." A newspaper reporter at the time of Tom Dula's death described her as "beautiful, but frail," and by *frail* he meant weak of character. When Laura's father realized she had disappeared in the night with his horse, he told neighbors he didn't care what happened to her, he just wanted his horse back. It is now thought that Tom Dula killed Laura Foster because he believed she had given him the pox—what we call syphilis. Laura was known for having "round heels," which meant she was easily tipped over, which meant she slept with a lot of men. Today we would call her a slut. There have always been names like that for women. In an Amazon review of a fictionalized version of the Tom Dula story, a reader writes, "I know that many folks from the area have taken offense to the portrayal of Laura Foster as less than the virginal victim of a crime of passion. But in this case, she was what she was." In other words, she deserved to die.

Two months before you were born, a CNN anchor covering the Steubenville rape case confessed on air that it had been "incredibly difficult, even for an outsider like me, to watch what happened as these two young men that had such promising futures—star football players, very good students—literally watch as they believed their lives fell apart." The anchor, Poppy Harlow, was talking about the rape convictions of Trent Mays and Ma'lik Richmond. The two high school students had undressed one of their classmates while she was passed-out drunk, taken pictures of her with their cell phones, stuck their fingers inside of her, and later showed all their friends. Then when you were five months old, the Italian version of *Vogue* released a series of cover photos meant to make terrorizing women look sexy. In each picture a woman is crouching in fear, is covered in blood, is dead, but is also sleek and fashionably dressed, while a man somewhere on the edge of the frame stalks her. Joan Didion once said that we tell ourselves stories in order to live. But how we tell them also orders our lives.

In the end, the real Tom Dula never cried. The sheriff erected the gallows from pine beams in an oil field near the train depot, and the town closed its taverns for the day of the hanging. When Tom arrived in a cart carrying his coffin and was given the chance to address the nearly one thousand people gathered to watch him die, he spoke for an hour. He told the story of his childhood, his family, his military career; he cursed God and those he claimed had lied at his trial; and he talked about the nation and its recent dissolution and reunification. At 2:24 p.m. Tom Dula stood on the cart with the noose around his neck and waited for the wheels to move. "This time tomorrow / Reckon where I'll be / Down in yonder valley / A-hanging on a white oak tree." He died on May 1, the same day you were born. I don't know why this feels like justice to me. But sometimes, at least, it does. I would invent a world of perfect stories for you if I could. A world stuffed full of harmless, powerful songs. But I am complicit, too. I know this. I would do anything to make you not cry.

MY STORY

Fact: I have a younger sister

Fact: My younger sister gave birth to a little girl two weeks before my oldest daughter was born.

Fact: The first time I tried to write about my younger sister and her daughter and my daughter, I wrote that her daughter—my niece—was born two months before my daughter. I calculated the time wrong. It wasn't intentional, but when my sister disputed other parts of my retelling of her life and my life, she cited that error as one of many reasons that I had no right to tell a story about her.

Except that she didn't put it that way. She said I had no right to tell her story. In fact she wrote, THIS IS NOT YOUR STORY in all caps.

Confession: I likely miscalculated the time between my daughter's birth and her daughter's birth because everything that happened during that time has somehow run together. I know

her daughter was born premature and that she was in the neo-
natal unit for some time, but during that time our daughter
was born and, frankly, after that I had a hard time keeping up
with what was going on with my sister and her daughter
because so much was going on with Marta and me and our
new baby girl.

I still regret that. Everyone else in my family flew out to see
my sister, to meet her new tiny baby, everyone except for me. I
was just five hours away. I could have driven up to see her. But
I was so tired. We both were so tired.

Fact: The first time I wrote this essay, I began with a story about
Marta's psychic, who predicted there would be a loss in our
family.

It's that loss, really, that my sister says I have no right to
write about, that she says is her story, not mine. And I understand that. I almost agree. So I'm going to try to write only
about her and about me, which is to say, about us.

Story: My sister was the first person in our family who I told I
was gay. In the story as I remember it, I was a junior in high
school and she was a freshman. She'd already asked me about
my sexuality once, when a friend of hers at church told her I
was a lesbian.

"That's a lie," I told her then, and we didn't speak about it
again for a year.

But then one night we went for a walk through the streets of
our Tampa suburb. Probably it was to take our dog out, though
maybe we just wanted to talk out of earshot of our mom. Our
neighborhood butted up against a swamp, and at night you
could hear the cicadas buzz and the occasional cry of an alligator. The air was thick with salt.

"Jenny said you were a lesbian yesterday, but I told her that wasn't true," my sister said out of nowhere, just as we were rounding the corner back toward our house. It was clear she was proud of the way she had defended me, and perhaps it was that fact that made me tell her the truth.

Afterward she was surprised for a moment. It was one of the few times I've shocked her. But she quickly recovered.

"This is great," she said. "I've got a lesbian sister."

Revision: My sister now says that I actually came out to her at the mall. And probably she's right. She has the best memory of all of us, even after all the drugs she's taken, even with her depression and anxiety, and the other drugs she's been given to keep all of that in check.

Story: When we were kids one of our favorite movies was *The Sound of Music*. We watched it again and again until we had parts of it memorized. "We can do it without help, father." Or "I'm far, far too outspoken. It's one of my worst faults." Or "When the Lord closes a door, somewhere he opens a window."

But my sister always remembered more lines than my brother or me, and eventually she knew the whole movie by heart. All two hours and fifty-four minutes of it. Then she did the same with *The Princess Bride*. And, after that, *The Fugitive*.

Quote: "I didn't kill my wife!"

Quote: "I don't care!"

Fact: *The Fugitive* is also about trying to get the story right. And in the end, it succeeds. He *didn't* kill his wife. The truth is exposed. The world made right.

Story: When I was a newspaper journalist, I was obsessed with getting the facts right. Once, I couldn't sleep because I'd written in an article that a boy's eyes were blue, and I was afraid that they were actually green. Finally I called the photographer and asked him to look. He said that they were brown.

I hung up with him and quickly called the copy desk and told them to change the eye color in my story from blue to brown. It was ten at night. The next day's paper was about to go to print. But they said they had time to make the change, and I hung up and went back to sleep, satisfied that I had gotten the facts right, which at that time meant to me that I had also gotten the story right.

But now I'm not so sure.

Story: My sister says that the first time I visited her in Minneapolis I joked that I was the "first reporter on the scene." I don't remember that. What I remember is that her hair smelled smoke and shampoo when we hugged and that I picked her up at a homeless shelter downtown and drove her to a sober house nearby to pick up her things. A young woman with tattoos covering her arms led us down to a basement where there were bags and bags of clothes from former residents strewn across the floor. While my sister looked for her favorite jacket, the woman told us how the saddest thing was when they had to throw out pictures of people's graduations or people's kids.

What I remember most about that day, though, was how afterward we went to St. Paul's Cathedral. It's the highest point in the city, and my sister said that when she first saw it she asked if it was a mountain. I said it was beautiful, and she said that once she and her boyfriend were making out on the corner and a guy from the church came up and said, "Um, can you do that somewhere else?"

"We told him we just wanted to see inside," my sister said. "And the guy got all happy and invited us in. I guess he wanted to save our souls."

And I laughed at that. Because the other thing about my sister is that she's really funny, and always in the most unexpected ways.

Joke: When they brought my sister home from the hospital, the first thing they say I said was, "Look at those pretty blue eyes." Then I jabbed two fingers at her eyes, which are the same dark blue as my own. Even today I can almost feel the swing of my arm, the thrust in my little fingers.

Someone caught me before they could land.

But then a year later my sister was in her baby walker in the kitchen, and my friend Safire and I pushed her down the stairs to the basement. Safire's mom was supposed to be watching us, but she was on the phone. My sister fell the entire flight and might have landed on her head at the bottom if there hadn't been a family friend there, rebuilding the banister. He caught her and she survived, and now the story is one we retell on holidays or when we introduce new lovers or friends to the family.

The joke goes that I tried to kill my little sister but failed. We all laugh.

Confession: The truth is that I was jealous of my sister for a long time. She was freer—still is freer—than me. As a kid she had red, curly hair and light freckles that made adults adore her. Once, an artist friend of my mom's asked if he could use us as models in a newspaper ad for an upcoming show of his paintings. He'd made T-shirts advertising his gallery, and our job was to put them on, pose, and look cute.

That year I wanted to be either an actress or a model, and in the hour before he came I carefully crimped and recrimped my hair to frizzy perfection. By the time he arrived I looked like I had been electrocuted. Meanwhile, my sister's curls bounced and her joie de vivre was as evident as my controlled smile. After taking a few shots of all of us, the artist asked if he could take some photos of my sister by herself. I still remember the feeling of slipping into the background while she took her place—beaming—before the lens.

Fact: When my sister told me she was pregnant, my first response was, "Are you going to keep it?"

Fact: That was two months after Marta found out she was pregnant.

Story: A few weeks later my sister sent an e-mail to the extended family.

"Greetings," she wrote. "For the sole purpose of producing grandchildren for my mom, I will be having a baby. We are looking forward to a June arrival of the little one. Mama and baby are healthy and happy."

My mom promptly sent out another e-mail announcing that Marta and I were also expecting a girl. Later she asked if I was jealous that my sister had once again stolen my thunder.

"Mom," I said. "That was over a long time ago. Now I just want her to be OK."

It was clear she didn't believe me.

Fact: My memory may be bad, but I'm good at is keeping a journal. Most of everything I pass off as remembered here or elsewhere is actually a retelling of something I once wrote down in my journal many years before.

For example: Two months after our daughter was born, I dreamed that she was suddenly too small, the size of a sparrow. We had gone to see a play, and I stepped out briefly from the darkness of one act and into the light of a kitchen to clean her up because she was suddenly dirty and wet and full of teeth. I held her under a stream of water that was pouring into a large industrial sink, but when the water hit her skin it created a suction between her body and the drain, and before I could stop it her limbs were being pulling downward with a force I couldn't counter. I eventually freed her, but I knew immediately she had been damaged. Her legs were distorted, and she had a pained look in her wide eyes. Marta showed up, and when I told her what had happened, her face was the absence of love. I explained why it wasn't my fault, but my story made no sense.

Fact: The same day, my sister told me that Child Protective Services had started coming to her apartment to check in on her, her boyfriend—now husband—and their little baby girl.

Quote: "Inconceivable!"

Fact: Seven months after that she lost custody of her daughter. It was the day before she, her husband, and my niece were going to fly out to Florida to see us for Christmas.

Quote: "Inconceivable!"

Quote: "Stop saying that!"

Confession: In my first version of this essay, I wrote a lot about why my sister lost custody of her daughter. I included lots of details about what she had maybe done or not done, according to what I had written in my journal at the time, but my sister now says that none of that is true.

But even given that, even given all that I wrote before, when I showed that essay to an editor once, her response was that she needed more.

"I still don't understand," she said. "What happened?"

Quote: "Less is more."

Story: I once visited one of Ludwig Mies van der Rohe's famous glass houses, one of his *less is more* designs. It was the one in Barcelona, at the foot of a large hill or mountain at the top of which is a museum dedicated to the sculptor Joan Miró. And now, as I am picturing the house and then the museum, I remember my sister there, too. I see us standing on each side of a glass wall, making faces at each other. I see us running up the hill toward the museum and standing before Miró's sculpture "The Carcass of a Bird" and asking each other what it means.

But I know that's a lie. Or a desired truth. I visited that house with my parents, not my sister. I was a junior in college at the time, and my sister—I don't even know where she was. As for the house, it wasn't entirely made of glass, though it is marked by its simplicity. It was built to represent a "continuous space," one in which the outside and inside run together.

Story: One of my last stories as a newspaper reporter was about corruption in the family courts in Houston. I spent weeks in those courts, listening to child custody testimonies and juvenile delinquency cases. And then I spent hours back at the office, analyzing a database of public attorney appointments and contributions by those same attorneys to the judges overseeing their cases—the same judges who would appoint those attorneys to represent clients too poor to hire their own.

I remember one case in particular: a mother with schizophrenia who had lost custody of her baby. For a while, at least, that woman's mother was taking care of the little boy. But then CPS realized that the grandmother was still letting her schizophrenic daughter see her child, and they came back to court to sever the grandmother's rights, too.

It was a heartbreaking story to witness, and yet writing it up for the paper was relatively easy. To be balanced and fair, I only had to get a quote from one side and a quote from the other and then find an expert somewhere to say something factual and true. It didn't matter that I thought the grandmother looked like a broken baby bird or that I had no idea if the boy should be with her or with his foster family—a nice suburban couple who claimed they were just trying to do what was right. What mattered was that I never, ever wrote what I thought.

Confession: Probably I wasn't even allowed to use the word *corruption* in my article on the family courts that eventually ran in the newspaper. In fact, almost nothing I've done in this essay so far would be allowed in a newspaper. Not that I'm being dishonest. But I am allowing myself to form an opinion here. I'm letting my subject in. And as soon as we do that, we can't really speak in facts.

Fact: I have no idea what it's like to lose custody of your child—though this is a fact that could always change. Twenty years ago, I could have lost custody to my daughter just for being who I am—or at least for loving who I love, and making such a show of it.

And even today I lose her in small ways all the time. Just the other day she was asked to draw a picture of things and people who are important to her, and she drew a bunch of circles that she said were fathers.

"But you don't have a father," I reminded her. "You have two moms."

"No, I don't," she said.

Argument: I have the right to tell this story.

Counterargument: This isn't a story, really. It's an essay about my story and about my version of my sister's story. It's an essay about our story. No—it's *my* essay about our story. Her essay about our story would look and sound and feel like a completely different thing. A thing with wings, maybe, instead of teeth.

Story: After my sister lost custody of her daughter, she and her husband flew out to Florida to see us for Christmas. My mom had already planned a party for her friends to meet both babies, and though we almost canceled it, in the end we didn't. Someone said it wouldn't be fair to me, and I unfairly agreed. I'm not sure why. All I know is that we decided to have it, and while it was starting, while people were holding our baby girl and Marta and I were there talking about our baby girl who was finally starting to sleep, at some point while Marta and I were smiling or laughing, my sister went upstairs to her old room and pasted a collage of photos of her daughter on a poster board. She wrote her daughter's name at the top of that collage and brought it down and put it on the couch, where it sat all afternoon like an empty nest. She seemed high at the time, but I'm sure she'll dispute that fact, and if she was, who could really blame her? I would have gotten high if I'd just lost my daughter and then flown out to a family gathering where everyone was trying to celebrate my sister's new daughter, where everyone was pretending that something terrible hadn't just happened. I would have fucking wanted to break every glass thing in that glass house.

Fact: I love my sister.

Fact: She's sober now. She wants you to know that.

Essay: I am trying to tell our story, but the only one I can tell is mine.

MY CHILD

ONE JANUARY DAY in 2011 a woman named Julie Schenecker picked up her thirteen-year-old son from soccer practice and shot him in the head as they were driving home. She then parked the family van in the garage, went upstairs, and shot her sixteen-year-old daughter at her desk.

The family lived in a winding subdivision in Tampa, Florida, a place called Tampa Palms, which was once just cow fields and swamp but in the 1980s began to be platted and subdivided and paved. There are now some fifteen thousand houses in a series of new subdivisions, including Tampa Palms, that make up what is known as New Tampa.

I know this because I grew up in Tampa Palms. We moved there when I was eleven, and my family stayed in the same house until I was twenty. Our house was just three miles from the Schenecker house. Theirs was in a neighborhood called Ashington Reserve. Ours was in a neighborhood called Tremont. All the neighborhoods in Tampa Palms had vaguely

British sounding names, as if by name alone we'd be tricked into seeing manors instead of swamp.

I don't know why I am writing about Julie Schenecker or reading so much recently about women who have killed their children. I am two months pregnant and expecting my second child, but the first that I will birth. Our daughter, who my wife had by C-section two years ago, is in the other room now pretending that she is me and that parts of the living room are different places we have lived in or visited.

The word for the killing of one's child is *filicide*. When it is a mother who does it, the term is *maternal filicide*. We all know cases like this. Andrea Yates is the most famous. She drowned five of her children in a bathtub in a Houston suburb in 2001. When I moved to that city in 2006 to work as a journalist, she was still on trial. The jury declared her innocent by reason of insanity that same year. She now lives in a mental institution in Texas, and for a while, at least, her roommate was a woman named Dena Schlosser, who killed her eleven-month-old daughter by cutting off her arms. These things are more common than we think.

This fall I am teaching a class on literary true crime at a university in West Texas, where I now live. We've read Truman Capote's *In Cold Blood*, Susan Orlean's *The Orchid Thief*, Lacy Johnson's *The Other Side*, and lots of other essays about crimes big and small. Each time we read something new, I ask my students the same question: What keeps us reading? With traditional crime stories, we keep reading to find out who did it, or whodunit. With literary true crime, though, the question that drives the narrative is not *who* did it, but *why* she did it.

I got pregnant midway through the semester. I am thirty-six, just past the age when they start to say fertility may be an issue. I'd been trying for three months and was beginning to think maybe they were right. Each month, after going in to be inseminated, I was sure it had worked. One month I felt extra tired, the next I had crazy dreams, and the next I couldn't stop crying. In the end, the crying was the true sign. It was followed by a small pimple on my nose, and then the inability to sleep, and finally a metallic taste in my mouth. By the time the little white strip declared me pregnant, I already knew. You realize when your body has been overtaken.

Growing up in Tampa Palms it was hard not to notice how recently everything around us had once been wild. Our backyard melted into what the developers called a *wildlife preserve*. Really it was miles and miles of thick, wet swamp that went from green to black the farther back you walked. Not that we ever walked that far. There was a sense then that we were, and always would be, only visitors there. No matter our cul-de-sacs or our community design standards or our sprawling country club down the road. It might take hundreds of years, but eventually the swamp would retake what it had lost. Once, while riding my bike on the sidewalk, I had to suddenly veer off the path because there was a baby alligator in my way. Another time, while waiting for the school bus, I watched the primordial body of a walking catfish flip across the pavement back toward a nearby man-made lake. And then there was the day our dog got loose and disappeared deeper into the swamp than we'd ever dared go. He came back that evening covered in a rancid, musty, fishy smell that ran so deep it took weeks to fully wash it out of him.

Every time a mother kills her child someone calls it the most unnatural of acts. But what no one seems to realize is that women have always killed their children. Why they do so is another question. Several hundred years ago women sometimes killed their children because they really wanted to kill themselves. The understanding of church law then was that a murderer who later confessed would go to heaven, but anyone who committed suicide would go to hell. Because infants and children were seen as innocent and therefore gained automatic entry into heaven, suicidal women would sometimes kill their children, or someone else's child, and then seek forgiveness before being put to death. The logic of their decision was sound, even if their choice seems unimaginable.

When we say unimaginable, of course, we don't mean that we can't imagine the act. We mean that we don't want to imagine it. Here I am writing about women who kill their children, and about this specific woman, this Julie Schenecker, who killed her two children, and I won't for one moment—even as a thought experiment—imagine any harm coming to my daughter. I will not imagine that because I do not want to imagine that—ever. That is why we say that these murders are unimaginable. We don't want to imagine that they happen or that they could happen to us. When I ask my students why we read books like *In Cold Blood*, they quite smartly say, "So that we can know that we are not murderers." But after a pause one of them adds, "Also, to remind us that we might have been, or could still be."

Most often when women kill their children, those children are babies, and most often we decide they did so because of what we now call postpartum depression. It is true that your body courses with strange, foreign-seeming hormones when you get pregnant, and it is true that those hormones can make you feel not like yourself, and so it is imaginable that for some women those hormones could make them do something they would never have thought themselves capable of before. But Julie Schenecker's children were already teenagers. She had been depressed, was being treated for bipolar disorder, and had drug and alcohol issues, but for a woman to kill her teenage children is still almost unheard of. When asked why she did it, Julie told police that her teenagers were being "mouthy."

Women give a lot of different reasons for killing their children. Andrea Yates said her kids were misbehaving and she was worried they would go to hell. She believed their transgressions were her fault, that she had been a bad mother, and killing them was the only way to rectify things. This past summer three different women in New York City killed their babies by throwing them out windows, and each gave a different reason why. One of them screamed, "We're all gonna die," before dropping her child to his death. Another told police that her one-month-old was possessed by an evil spirit, and she was trying to stop his pain. The final woman threw her baby out the window soon after giving birth. She had been trying to hide her pregnancy for months and most likely never wanted the child to begin with.

I should clarify at this point that I have never thought about killing my child. This essay isn't leading toward that sort of reveal. I was not ready to become a mother when Marta told me she wanted to get pregnant, but I've adjusted to being one, and I love our daughter with an intensity I've never felt for anyone before. I wonder sometimes, though, if I will feel differently about the son or daughter I am growing inside me now. I already sense a more animalistic connection. My body feels possessed. I am tired nearly all the time, and I've suddenly fallen in love with classical music, especially Bach. Before, classical music was just noise—I liked music with lyrics, with a guitar—but these days if I hear the Goldberg Variations, I begin to weep and feel like something almost godly is consuming me, and I don't believe in God. I can't imagine, then, that I won't love this baby when he or she arrives. But I also can't imagine that this baby will some day be its own being and no longer be a part of me.

I wrote a letter to Julie Schenecker once. Reading it over now, I realize that I wrote mostly about myself. I suppose I thought that might help distract her. She had just been found guilty of murder and was given a life sentence. "Dear Julie Schenecker," I wrote, "I am writing because I thought you'd like to get a letter or two from someone outside of prison. I've read about your story in the newspapers, but I of course know nothing about you." I then told her about living in Tampa Palms and now in West Texas. I explained that I am a new mom, that my daughter likes baby dolls, Sesame Street characters, and forks, and that just that week she learned to count to three. Then I wrote a little bit about where we live—how everything is flat in West Texas and how we're ringed by oil derricks and cotton fields and how the only real attraction is the prairie dogs, who all give birth in the spring. "I have no idea if you welcome mail or not, but if you would benefit from a correspondence with someone, feel free to write me back," I said in closing. "I assume—though this is me projecting—that you must feel rather isolated at this point. If you prefer not to write, I hope you take this letter as a sign that not all the world thinks ill of you."

Julie never responded, but I later watched an interview she gave to a TV journalist named Sabrina Fazan, who also wrote to her in prison. Fazan sent Julie letters regularly, every month over a period of four years, before Julie finally agreed to be interviewed. Sabrina opens the segment by explaining her persistence to viewers: "Like so many of you, I wanted answers, not just as a journalist, but as a mother," she says. Then we cut to the footage of Julie in a large, empty room, sitting on a chair with her head bowed. Her hair is long and unbrushed, and she keeps wiping away tears. When she talks, her voice sounds like a child's. You notice the wrinkles around her eyes and how her mascara smears. She says she doesn't regret killing her children. She says she saw their souls go up to heaven when they died and that she hopes to join them there soon. At one point in the interview, her voice grows harsh. "I don't understand what happened that day," she says, staring at Sabrina. "So I don't know how to make *you* understand what happened that day."

One day in class we are talking about *In Cold Blood*, and one of my students gets angry. She says she is frustrated with how Truman Capote keeps making her feel sorry for Perry Smith, a man who broke into the house of a rural Kansas family and shot and killed four people: first the father, then the fifteen-year-old son, then the sixteen-year-old daughter, and finally the mother. Several other students agree. What they want, they say, is to feel for the *real* victims. I listen and then I talk about the value of ambiguity, how not ever knowing for sure is what makes something art. But the truth is, I understand what they mean. If I consider, for even a moment, Julie Schenecker's children, it is hard for me to keep telling her story. Her daughter went to my high school. She was in the same magnet program as I was and probably had some of the same teachers. She ran cross-country, just like I did, and she loved to read. I remember when I was sixteen, how the world still seemed not fully formed. And then I try to imagine my mother standing over me at my desk with a gun in her hand.

It is difficult to know exactly how many women kill their children each year. One researcher found around one hundred cases in the United States over a ten-year period, but others say the figure may be closer to two hundred a year. The problem is one of classification. A child killed because of neglect is not the same as a child killed purposely by its mother or father. And an abandoned baby is also not the same as a thirteen-year-old shot in the head by his mother on the way home from soccer practice—even though the root cause may sometimes be the same.

There have been, of course, a number of attempts at classification. One of the first systems, established in 1925, broke women down into two groups: those who were lactating when they killed their children and those who weren't. Women who fell into the first group were thought to have killed because of either exhaustion or something called "lactation psychosis." In another classification system, researchers labeled women based on whether they killed their first child or a subsequent one and on how ethical or sexual they were "by nature." One of the most influential—but still faulty—systems was established by a man named Phillip Resnick in the 1960s and '70s. Compiling reports of children and babies killed by their mothers between 1751 and 1968, he came up with a list of five different types of filicide: altruistic, acutely psychotic, unwanted child, accidental, and spousal revenge. The most common type by far was altruistic, meaning that the mother believed her actions were meant to help her child.

Though often mumbling or incoherent in her taped interview,

Julie has a few moments where she speaks clearly, even if the words she says still make little sense. In one of those moments she says that the reason she killed her kids was to protect them: her son from sexual abuse and her daughter from rape and mental illness. Julie tells Sabrina Fazan that she was raped when she was younger. The implication seems to be that she wanted to protect her children from the violence that she suffered as a younger woman as well as the mental illness that so obviously debilitates her now. Fazan is quick to point out that there are no police reports of Julie having been raped as a young girl or woman, but I can't help but think that's beside the point.

Julie grew up in a small Iowa town called Muscatine that is only an hour from the town where Marta and I met and where, three years later, our daughter was born. Iowa, like everywhere, was once wild terrain—prairie instead of swamp—but that has now been replaced by small towns and cornfields. Julie played volleyball for Muscatine High School and was smart and popular, the kind of person "you secretly wanted to be," said an old friend. After the murders became national news, two Tampa reporters went to visit Julie's hometown to interview its residents and afterward referred to it as "small, nondescript" in the article they wrote up. The editor of Julie's hometown newspaper took issue with that description, calling it cliché and lazy, and wrote in a subsequent editorial that small towns are where we go to be safe. One Muscatine resident wrote in to agree: "Maybe, I wish that Julie would have stayed. Maybe, things would be different for her now."

That's a human tendency: to think of what could have been different or would have been different, *if only*. In class my students say, if only Perry's mother hadn't been an alcoholic. If only his father were kinder. If only he had found God instead of turning back to crime. In life we say, if only Julie had stayed in Iowa. If only her husband, a colonel in the Army, had not gone overseas and left her alone with the two kids. If only she had not quit her important job as a Russian linguist for the Army to stay home with those kids after they were born. If only she had never become a mother in the first place.

When researching Julie, the photos are the hardest part to stomach—and I am not taking about the images of dead bodies or blood splatter. I am talking about the photos from inside what really looks like an ordinary suburban house. There is a picture of Julie with her children when she looks much younger: blonde and smiling and wealthy. There are pictures of a calendar with notes about what is planned for the future: a sports physical, a yard sale. It is the ordinariness of everything that feels particularly sad. This could be anyone's house. This could have been ours.

In our house, a small black-and-white photo of my first ultrasound hangs on the fridge. The baby was only the size of a lentil at that point. It was not even really anything, and yet when we first saw his or her heart fluttering on the screen, I was surprised by how much it affected me. Marta and I held hands and watched it, and I had to resist the urge to beg the technician to stay on that image just a little bit longer. The print we have now, so static and still, does not capture what it feels like in that moment—seeing the smallest fluttering of life inside you. *That's mine*, I thought. *That is mine.*

And so when we go in for our second ultrasound today, we are mostly just giddy to see the heartbeat again. We have already named him or her Jeremiah. It's a silly name we don't intend on using, but we like having something to call this thing that is growing inside me. Except that when the ultrasound technician puts the wand on my belly, she can't find the heartbeat at first. She says my uterus is oddly shaped and decides to try it vaginally, like they did before. But when she checks that way, we can see the baby, and still there is no fluttering. I keep waiting as she moves the wand around inside me, looking at my ovaries, at the lining of my uterus. I keep waiting for her to say something, but she only confirms that there's no heartbeat when I ask.

Back home, I say I am going for a run, and I put on my shoes and run through our barren West Texas streets where everything everywhere seems to be turning brown in preparation for winter. Tampa is so hot and wet that at times it feels very much like a heartbeat, so aflutter with change and growth. West Texas, by contrast, is dry and empty and feels slow moving. I have to remind myself that it, too, was once open land and wild growth. The Comanche ran horses and buffalo across its high plains for hundreds of years until farmers from the East Coast moved in, killed off the buffalo, and replaced the prairie with cotton farms. Nothing is natural or unimaginable. Even the few sycamore and oak trees that I so love in our West Texas neighborhood are not native to this area. They were planted here years ago by the city's founders to make this place seem livable.

They tell me this is called a missed miscarriage, which means that the baby inside me has died, but my body refuses to recognize that fact. It still thinks I am pregnant and might continue to think so for weeks. These things happen sometimes; our bodies can be tricked just like we can. But either way, the baby has died, and when I run, it is there—its heart no longer fluttering while mine beats on, a deafening drum in my ears. This is not something I imagined happening, though I should have. And though I know I shouldn't—in fact the doctor warned me not to—I keep thinking that I am somehow responsible: that flight I took a week ago to go to a conference or the sliced turkey meat I ate before reading online that I shouldn't. *If only.* I do not feel now like I want to understand Julie Schenecker. I feel angry with her for the first time. She had two children, and she killed them.

My daughter is at a stage now in which she wants to be a mother. She has several dolls, but, really, she will make anything into her baby. She has cradled a fork. She has cradled a squeegee. She has pulled an eggplant from the fridge and wrapped it in her arms and rocked it to sleep. I watch her as she pretends to be me, or someone like me, and I am reminded of that famous baby monkey experiment on the mother-child bond, how the baby monkeys would cling to a cloth replica of a mother even when offered a wire replica holding a bottle of milk. The conclusion seemed to be that maternal bonds are important, a fact doubted in the 1950s. But a better conclusion to me is that we can make a mother out of anything—even nature, even the earth—if we want one badly enough. Just like my daughter sits here beside me and makes her very own baby out of what someone less dedicated could easily mistake for the luminous purple fruit of a nightshade.

MY RETURN

RETURNING TO IOWA, everything is the same, but also everything isn't. It's still summer, and the car is still packed. There is still that "Fields of Opportunity" billboard we pass at the border on Highway 218 welcoming us to Iowa. There is still the sense of having made a right decision. We left the rain behind in Missouri, and now Marta is driving while I sit in the back seat beside our daughter, trying to entertain her on the final stretch of this three-day road trip from Texas, where we live now, to Iowa, where we'll live again, if only for the summer.

"This is where you were born," I tell our daughter. "This is your real home."

But she's three, so instead of responding she asks, "What's that?" A bowling alley beside an open field. And, "What's that?" The Iowa River streaming past a power plant. And, "Are we in Lubbock?"

When I first drove here I was alone—alone with Finn. In those days it was him I talked to, those days before having a wife, then a child, and now another child growing inside me—a baby whom I also talk to when we're alone, in a way that feels similar to how I used to talk to Finn. This is the second baby I've carried. The first I lost last fall. This is the second time I've moved to Iowa. The first time feels so long ago.

The first time it was late summer, and I had also left Missouri behind. I also saw that billboard about Iowa's fields of opportunity, which made me laugh.

"Maybe it's a sign," I told Finn.

I had left behind a lot on that trip north: a well-paying job in Houston, a relationship, and, also, all my furniture and most of my belongings, save some rugs and blankets wrapped around framed pictures and maps of other places I'd lived and left.

I was moving to Iowa because I thought I needed a change. Finn was in the front seat beside me, his sleek, black head reaching out the window to pant as we reached the last stop sign before pulling up to what would be my new home: a blue, two-story house I had found on Craigslist, a house I would share with three other roommates I had also found on Craigslist: a musician, a playwright, and a sculptor.

My plan was to rebuild a life just like that—via the Internet and thrift stores. I would build myself a bed out of foam-core doors I found at a construction resale shop. I would buy a new bike at a garage sale and find new pots and pans at the auction. I would move my online dating profile from Texas to Iowa, mark myself single, and add that I listen to a lot of Tom Waits and have an unusually long neck.

When we pulled up to my new house that day and I opened the door, Finn dashed out in a streak of black and bounded up onto the front porch, sniffing the corners and doorstop with the dutiful confidence of the newly arrived. After declaring it satisfactory, he looked back, still panting, and waited for me to climb the steps and join him there.

The house we're staying in this summer belongs to one of those Craigslist roommates, the sculptor named Erica who just got married and is now one of my best friends. She and her boyfriend, now husband, bought this house when it was condemned. They spent four years rebuilding it: carpeting the rooms upstairs, rewiring the cables, planting a garden, hanging a front porch.

And when they were done they got married and went on a honeymoon road trip. While they're gone, they're letting us stay here. And while we're here in Iowa City, where Marta and I met, fell in love, and had our daughter, we're going to pretend we actually live in this town again, where we both still feel at home.

In the mornings I drop our daughter off at a farm day care, and Marta and I work at our respective desks, writing and reading. In the afternoons we go to the farmer's market or the pool or the public library. At night we invite over old friends for dinner. We've started playing Memory at the kitchen table, and usually Marta wins. When the sun goes down we read our daughter books until she falls asleep, and, if we have the energy, Marta and I watch something together on Netflix, or, even more rarely, we might make love.

We know this is not like it used to be, even though we are back where we were before. Because neither of us is who we were before. But we're still happy to be here. And within a few weeks it begins to feel like my friends' renovated house is actually ours and that this life we're inhabiting for the summer is also ours for keeps. Except that our daughter keeps asking from the back seat when we drive around, "Are we in Lubbock?" Or less often, "Is this Iowa City?"

My first time in Iowa City I spent my mornings alone, drinking coffee and reading through the postings from an e-mail list called Freecycle, an online group made up of people giving stuff away and others willing—or hoping—to take on that stuff for free.

I was searching for offers of furniture, winter clothes, or a desk. But I only ever found things I didn't need: a stamp collection kit, a Tupperware Jell-O mold, three red-eyed tetra fish, a pearly-pink conch shell listed beside the query, "Feeling the need to call Poseidon?"

The morning I arrived in Iowa, a woman named Candace was giving away a nearly full bag of Purina diabetic cat food, a post she concluded with three exclamation points, and by that afternoon she had returned, offering a jumbo pack of Pampers and coupons for Enfamil baby formula, this time with just one exclamation point.

In the days that followed I unpacked, bought Finn some new chew toys, and went to get my new University ID. Meanwhile, Candace offered up one baby stroller, an almost full container of Herbalife Cookies and Cream shake mix, and a George Foreman Grill. In return, she asked if anyone had the *Weight Watchers Complete Food and Dining Out* book, confiding that she planned to start dieting that week.

I was fascinated by the way her posts could construct a life, or, at least by how I convinced myself I could construe a life based on the posts of this woman I didn't know. I pictured her in her mid-thirties, hair bleached to the sheen of corn silk, just a few pounds plump of shapely, with feet that turned out slightly penguin-style when she walked. She seemed stable in a way I didn't feel then. And for a little while she was frozen like that: this caricature of a self-sufficient Midwestern mother I had invented to fill this flat Midwestern landscape I was coming to know.

But then, two days before my classes began, Candace posted again, and her offer this time was for "Ashley," her six-year-old, loyal, and mostly housebroken Jack Russell–Rat Terrier mix.

"We have a six-month-old son that is allergic to both our cat (which we are also trying to get rid of) and our dog!" she wrote. "I am extremely upset that I have to post this ad . . . but I have to for the sake of my little boy."

That same week I lost Finn for the first time. I was attending a new graduate-student teacher training—learning how best to teach Iowa students Shakespeare and ways to handle their Midwestern tendency to avoid dissension—when I got a call from a stranger who said he'd found my dog wandering the streets and that he was taking him to the pound. When I arrived for him an hour later, Finn's muzzle was wet with nervous drool, and he had a temporary pink leash around his neck. I distracted myself from crying on the drive back by lecturing Finn about the importance of staying close to home. But that afternoon, back at the training session, I cried despite myself when another graduate student showed a clip from the movie *In Her Shoes* in which Cameron Diaz reads Elizabeth Bishop's poem "One Art" to a blind man.

"The art of losing's not too hard to master," Diaz reads Bishop. "Though it may look like (*Write* it!) like disaster."

Finn was a mixed breed, just like Ashley, only he had the lithe body of a pointer and the energy of a black Lab. He'd found me while I was running through the streets of Houston, and, up until recently, he was the only thing I never gave away.

I've always been a runner, but back in Iowa this summer I no longer run. Pregnancy stole my energy in the early months, and, now that I have my stamina back, my body feels too rounded and off-center to run, so I walk instead. Every morning while Marta eats breakfast with our daughter, I go out alone to walk Iowa City's neighborhoods, and though I don't tell anyone, it's my favorite part of the day—just like running with Finn used to be my favorite moment of those days.

It's been raining a lot this summer—much more than when

we lived here before—and so I often pass over small bridges spanning swollen creeks, and I love the way our movements intersect at that point, me walking across their running waters. I like, too, when chance takes me past someone else walking or running a dog. I've never been good at approaching strangers, so usually I don't pet these dogs, but I want to with my whole body. This is another change that's come with pregnancy. When I want something, my desire doesn't stem from a small concentrated spot in my heart or stomach or groin; instead, it overtakes me. And when I see dogs walking with their owners, I want to pet them with such an intensity that, when in the end I don't, I walk away feeling bowed with loss.

The desire began recently while we were having dinner with some friends here that Marta knew from before. They're a younger couple with two daughters, just like we will soon have, and they also have a small, black puppy who looks a lot like Finn did a long time ago. I should have been playing with the kids or talking to Marta's friends that night, but instead I spent most of the evening wrestling and then snuggling their new puppy. When it was time to go, I kept making excuses to stay just a little longer, to pet her furry wriggling body just one more time. She was so soft and eager to be loved.

I knew why I was doing that, of course. But it was still surprising. It had been seven months since Finn died and five months since I got pregnant again after the miscarriage. I had thought I'd come to accept the exchange by now: a loss for a gain, or two losses for a gain. But, of course, it's never that simple.

I've wondered sometimes why I grew so attached to Candace in my first few months in Iowa. I know I have a habit of that: latching on to the lives of strangers and using them to try to understand my own life. I watch people in airports, I read the classifieds, I eavesdrop when the opportunity arises.

In some ways Candace felt to me like a parallel life. Like she was who I could have been, if only I would stay put. Even after I had all the stuff I needed, I kept checking Freecycle because I wanted to know what would happen to her—to her pets, her son, her stuff.

A couple of days after she posted about Ashley, the dog, Candace returned with an ad for her cat, Chooey, whom she was also giving away because of her baby boy's allergies. She repeated her story for those who hadn't been reading since the beginning.

"She is a very good cat and has never given us any reason to get rid of her," Candace told us, "which is why we are upset!"

The leaves began to turn, and Candace posted to ask if anyone had an aquarium for her family's new pet salamander—which she called the "perfect replacement pet." A week later she offered us the baby bathtub her son had just outgrown and asked if anyone had a toddler bath chair.

About midway through the semester, just as I was settling in and beginning to make friends, Candace posted again about Ashley. She said her dog had found a new home, though not through Freecycle. Her parents had agreed to take in the Terrier mix, which was good news, she wrote, because now her son would grow up knowing the dog that could have been his.

Winter fell, my first in Iowa, and I decided to write Candace. I couldn't know then that within six months I would meet Marta, or that, less than three years later, we would marry and Marta would give birth to our first child, or that, three months after that, we would move away from Iowa for good.

What I knew then was that after so much investment in a stranger's life, I wanted closure—or maybe contact. I wanted to know how it would end.

"I know this is a little late," I wrote to Candace, "but I

wondered if you found a home for Chooey the cat? I have a friend who isn't on Freecycle but is thinking about adopting a cat and wants to take one that really needs a home."

It was a lie, of course. I had no such friend, but it was the only excuse I could think of to write and ask this stranger about her life.

When Candace finally replied, her message was short and, as always, upbeat.

"Chooey found a new, loving home a couple of months ago," she gushed before adding, "Good luck in your search!"

Rebecca Solnit once wrote that places are more constant than people can ever be. Friedrich Nietzsche proposed the idea of eternal return: that time cycles rather than runs straight toward the horizon. Milan Kundera claimed that dogs link us to paradise.

I think about this baby growing inside me sometimes and the place she's in now. They say that after birth we're left with the constant desire to return, that in utero is our only time in paradise, the only moment when every need is met and nothing has yet been lost.

With Finn I was most at home on the road. We probably took a dozen road trips in our time together. We slept in a rest stop in my Subaru outside a Louisiana swamp. We stayed in cabins and houses and tents and, more than once, in the bed of a woman I was sure I would soon learn to love. We drove up to see my sister after she got out of rehab and down to see my mom after her mom died.

For our final trip, when I took Finn to the vet to be put down, Marta offered to go with me, but I said I wanted to be alone. He'd been sick for at least a year by then. I was pregnant for the first time, not yet aware that the fetus's heartbeat was about to stop.

On the drive to the vet's office, I talked to Finn the whole way. I told him that I loved him and that he would always be my best friend. He was in the back, lying on my daughter's duck towel, which I'd put there to soak up the urine he could no longer keep from leaking out of him.

The woman at the front desk checked us in, and while we waited to be called I stroked his soft ears and told him how glad I was to have found him, that he had found me.

After they injected him with a liquid that would make his heart stop, they left me alone with him, and I watched as his eyes turned blue and then, slowly, became glass. I felt his chest, and his heart was still there, moving like the smallest of babies. Until it wasn't, and I left.

We walk to an old friend's house for dinner on one of our last nights in town, and there is a woman walking her dog in front of us. It has finally stopped raining here, and Iowa City looks just like it used to, even though I know it isn't the same. My daughter asks about the dog in front of us and then adds, "Where is our dog?"

"Don't you remember?" I say, my voice not quite my own. "Finn got old and he was sick, and sometimes when animals get old and sick, they die. He's not ours anymore."

We've told her this story before, probably a dozen times. But she never seems to remember, or at least she doesn't remember what it means.

Three-year-olds see the world like that. We are in both Lubbock and Iowa City. Today is yesterday, and tomorrow could be next summer. We once had a dog named Finn and we still have him. He's just not ours anymore.

coda

When it happened, I suddenly recalled the expression: *split in two.*

It was six in the morning, and I had been laboring for twelve hours. The sun was almost up. We had the youngest, blondest night nurse, who was sweet like I imagine angels must be. "You're doing incredible," she would tell me as she pulled her hand out from inside me and announced how wide I had become. Six centimeters, then eight, then nine, then nine and a half. I had Marta on one side and our doula on the other. The lights were dimmed, the bathroom door ajar, and a row of windows ran curtainless before the night sky. We would be calm, or at least recovering, and I might gasp, exhale, and say how long or how strong the last one had been, my feet bare and still trembling, and then the next one would start to form inside, rolling me up just as it stretched me to the corners of the room. It was not pain any more than it was euphoria. It permeated my body, my vision, the space between my self and everything else. So much so that there were moments when I was sure I could talk to God. And, if you'll remember, I don't believe in him. But there was an otherworldliness to my laboring that made it seem like he very well could exist, like that would be the least fantastical of all the glorious and mad things that were happening between me and the absoluteness of pain. But then the baby came, and I was split in two, and the baby ate whatever there was of God in the room, and now he definitely doesn't exist.

Split in two is redundant. If you split anything, you create two. Imagine a fruit. An apple maybe. It's been dropped from a good height, and on impact it breaks into halves. To make new life, the cells first divide. Marta told me that when she saw our daughter come out of me part of me came out with her. It was not pretty. I still wish I had seen it.

Two weeks to the day after the birth, we had an election. There was a man on one side and a woman on the other. He was tall and spoke in simple sentences. She was more or less his age, and perhaps they could have been a couple in some other universe, one in which he and she grew up to be ordinary people, like you and I are, and met and fell in love, he attracted to her decisive personality and great hair, she to his height and refusal ever to back down. And, in a world like that, one in which they would never realize their potential—the potential in them to galvanize all that is mean and ugly about the rest of us living in this country where we are forever and always choosing between just two options, neither always all that good—in a world like that, they might have just been happy, or at least content, to marry and have kids and watch their kids grow and then retire and eventually die.

I was on her side, of course. And the night the election results came in, I was in the same spot in our bed where I had been most of every day since the birth, since my splitting in two. I nursed her, our new little one—just seven pounds, mouth a whirlpool, hands like crocuses breaking earth—and my nipples cracked and bled. At night they leaked milk into my sleeping shirt, and I'd wake sticky and bleary-eyed to feed her more. But I was bliss-ful—full of bliss. Because there is a rush of hormones after birth and then waves of endorphins for weeks after that, every time I looked at her, fed her, smelled her, thought of her. It seemed that nothing could ever go wrong. It appeared that the world was perfectly planned. Everything made sense and had its place.

But I was also blissful because I believed things could only keep getting better. Everything I read told me that my candidate would win. My newspaper predicted her with ninety percent surety. Friends were explaining to their little girls how tomorrow they would wake up—finally—to a woman in the White House.

And so there Marta and I were, in the bed, with this tiny one who had just a week before been part of me. I think she'd just fallen asleep, though she could have been awake and feeding, and we were watching the election returns. Indiana and Ken-tucky for him. Vermont for her. West Virginia, South Carolina, Alabama: his. Connecticut and Delaware: hers. It was around nine that I started to realize this country, my country, might actually choose him. But I thought if I closed my eyes maybe I would wake later to find that everything was as it should be, as I wanted it to be. My baby was already asleep, and so I slept, too. When she woke me up at three to feed, he had won Iowa and Florida, and an hour later when she conceded I realized that we'd been split, too.

I also realized that we've always been split.

There was an interactive graphic put up by the *Wall Street*

Journal sometime before the election that showed the Facebook feeds of conservatives and liberals. You could search by issue. I searched the shooting at Orlando's Pulse nightclub, and the liberal feeds were all about safe spaces and hate crimes and queer and Latinx culture and what gay clubs have meant to those of us who still are not able to show affection in public without some degree of fear. And the conservative feeds were all about terrorism and ISIS and domestic radicalization and the "clash of civilizations" and the fact that the liberals refused to call Omar Mateen an Islamic terrorist.

I remembered how I felt when Orlando happened. I was five months pregnant then. She might not have even survived on her own at that point. We were not yet two. I woke up early that morning to her moving inside me, and, unable to fall back asleep, I read the news and learned that a twenty-nine-year-old man had walked into the Pulse nightclub in Orlando and killed forty-nine people before he was shot by police. I had just come back from living in Orlando for the winter. I had its warmth and strip malls on my skin, on my breath, still. And I was crying before I even realized I was crying, tears that felt like they had no beginning, but have always been there, at the lip of my eyes, waiting.

When I saw that infographic about Facebook feeds, the sadness was similar to what I would later feel after the election. It is the kind of sadness you might feel for a lost limb, or for the baby inside you whose heart has stopped before she ever really began. In the days after the election, there were new Facebook feeds, new stories: "Make America White Again" and "Go Home" spray-painted on cars and walls. A man threatening to light a Muslim woman on fire unless she removed her hijab. Students or friends or friends of friends who were afraid to go out in the world, afraid to go to school, or even a convenience store. And then there were the celebrations: that man yelling at all the passengers on a Delta flight from Atlanta to Allenton, Pennsylvania, "He's your president, every goddamn one of you. If you don't like it, too bad."

We never really own our country, not in the way we think we own ourselves, these shimmering bodies that hold us. Before the birth, what I had was a belly. It was beautiful and round, and I liked to place my hands on it and rub. I rubbed because I loved the way I was expanding, and I wanted to feel my expansion as well as see it. It was mine. Until it wasn't.

This country is still mine, as much as it never was. We were of two minds—another expression that makes little sense. But it is true that there are some of us who are scared and some who feel calmer when he tells us that he will protect us, assures us that there is a clear enemy. Just over the border, just across the ocean, right here next to you. Beware.

I go today to see a radiologist. I found a lump while breastfeeding. Because while breastfeeding you end up touching your breasts more than you normally would, and one morning when I was kneading my breasts to see how full with milk they were, how much they would produce for this little being who needs me to live, I came upon the smallest of nodes, but a definite node, within the tissue. And in the weeks since, it's gotten bigger, and I have an appointment today to find out if it might kill me.

Or if it's benign—a word that's always sounded to me exactly like what it means: no harm, no need to fear. Today I will find out if that part of me is or isn't of me. I imagine if I could summon up a god again, I might feel less afraid.

Instead, I will finish writing this. This coda of sorts. Coda is from the Latin word for *tail*. In Spanish the word is *cola*. At the end of *One Hundred Years of Solitude*, a child is born with a tail, thus fulfilling the matriarch's original fear. She worried that one day her family would become too close, so close that they could no longer separate brother from sister from husband from wife, person from pig. And as is the case with all fears, hers eventually manifests itself.

That apple I mentioned before: I hadn't realized that it might lead us to Eve. We could also follow it to Newton—it was falling, after all. But the thing I like about Eve is that, in the story of the beginning of everything, it was she who gave us pain during birth. I want to thank her for that.

This is not pretty. But I am here to see it.

I have given up a dog and a home and a past and a country and a tiny fetus that might have been a baby. And I have gained a new home and a partner and a child and then another child and also a new life. Once, I was sitting on a dock looking at the tanned feet of my best friend while Florida's sun beat down on our backs. Everything I owned has since been lost. Even my memories are not the same. I can't know how long that round node in my breast has been mine. Maybe forever. My grandmother found a lump after dreaming that she would and, waking, there it was. We repeat the past just as the past becomes us.

And these little ones. Ours. Mine. How long will it take until I give up and admit that nothing I want so badly to own belongs to me. Least of all, this fleetingly small and insignificant life.

ACKnOWLEDGemenTS

I've heard it said that writing a book is like birthing a child, and that metaphor has always seemed both apt and completely off base. But one important similarity, for me, is this: I never could have done it by myself. There may be some authors who can wander off alone, squat, and birth a book in silent serenity, but I am not one of them. I needed help, and so thank you to those who have been my midwife, doctor, doula, nurse and—even occasionally—anesthesiologist.

For giving me the time and space in which to write this book, I want to thank all my university families over the years—including the university of Iowa, Texas Tech University, and, now, Arizona State University—as well as the generous folks at the Kerouac House in Orlando, Florida. And for allowing what I wrote to move from a Dropbox folder on my computer to an actual physical printing press, I will forever be grateful to judge Andre Dubus III and editors Joe Mackall and Dan Lehman at *River Teeth*, and to everyone at the University of New Mexico Press. In addition, thanks to the dedicated editors at those literary journals who have accepted, published, and championed my writing over the years.

For encouraging me to write in the first place, I am grateful to Amelia Bird, Dennis Covington, Kerry Howley, Claudia Kolker, Robert Strozier, and, many moons ago, Michael Smith, and Nicole Frugé. And for reading and giving me feedback on this specific book, a moon-size thanks to Curtis Bauer, Kathleen Blackburn, Katie Cortese, Jill Patterson, and, last but not at all least, Lina Maria Ferreira Cabeza-Vanegas. Thanks to my friends and fellow writers of LPG for reading my work, refilling my glass, and reminding me of the importance of community. And thanks to my family of birth, especially my mom and sister, for being honest, understanding, and fierce in your love—for your individual stories and for our shared ones.

Finally, I never would have written any of this, let alone finished it, without my family now: my daughters, who remind me daily why storytelling is indispensable, and my wife Marta, who reads everything I write, tells me when it's rubbish, tells me when she loves it, and believes in me no matter what. *Te quiero*, Marta.

Earlier versions of these essays appeared in the following literary journals:

The Pinch: "My Murderer's Futon"
The Toast: "My Catch" (published as "A Tremendous Fish")
Narrative.ly: "My Choice" (published as "What Happens
    When a Lesbian Reporter Covers a Pray-the-Gay-Away
    Convention")
Normal School: "My Hands" (published as "Wolf Biter")
Colorado Review: "My Namesake"
Gettysburg Review: "My Narrative Transformation" (published
    as "The Omnitrix")
Iowa Review: "My Language" (published as "Advise Me")
The Morning News: "My Wife" (published as "How to
    Unmarry Your Wife")
storySouth: "My Ballad for You"

Additionally, earlier versions of these essays appeared in the
following anthologies:

"My Hands" (published as "Wolf Biter"): in *Beautiful Flesh:
    A Body of Essays*, ed. Stephanie G'Schwind (Boulder:
    University Press of Colorado, 2017)
"My Return" (published as "Some Notes on Our Cyclical
    Nature"): in *This is the Place : Women Writing about Home*,
    ed. Margot Kahn and Kelly McMasters (Berkeley, CA: Seal
    Press, 2017).